# 50 WORSHIP IDEAS FOR SMALL GROUPS

**Donated by Methsoc**
**April 2005**

# 50 Worship Ideas for Small Groups

**STUART TOWNEND**
WITH
**MORGAN LEWIS**

KINGSWAY PUBLICATIONS
EASTBOURNE

First published 2000

Unless otherwise indicated, biblical quotations are
from the New International Version © 1973, 1978, 1984
by the International Bible Society.

Verses marked NASB are from
New American Standard Bible © The Lockman Foundation
1960, 1962, 1963, 1968, 1971, 1973, 1975, 1977.

ISBN 0 85476 872 6

Published by
KINGSWAY PUBLICATIONS
Lottbridge Drove, Eastbourne, BN23 6NT, England.
E-mail: books@kingsway.co.uk

Designed and produced for the publishers by
Bookprint Creative Services, P.O. Box 827, BN21 3YJ, England.
Printed in Great Britain.

# *Contents*

# *Acknowledgements*

The authors would like to thank the following people for their ideas and encouragement: Gwenda Lewis; Kate Simmonds; David Fellingham; Sarah Lewis; Caroline Townend; Catherine Townend; Sharon Barden; Elaine Evans.

# Introduction

If you've picked this book up because you feel you're struggling to lead worship in your small group, then let me assure you – you are not alone! While many churches seem to be moving ahead confidently and skilfully in Sunday morning congregational worship, I regularly hear small-group leaders confess that the worship in their midweek house group is pretty dull and lifeless by comparison.

I've been in a few small groups in my time. The worship times have ranged from pretty good to completely dire (I've actually *led* worship at both ends of the spectrum, too). The worst experience was being in a group of six women and one other man – who happened to be loud, enthusiastic, and completely tone deaf. We had no instruments, and our rendition of the two-part chorus of 'God of glory' still wakes me up in a cold sweat.

Why does small-group worship so often seem to be a struggle? Many reasons are offered: lack of musicians, people are tired after a day's work, the room's too small, the sofa's too comfortable, and so on. But I think there's a more fundamental reason – *no one's shown us how to do it.*

**Sunday morning/Wednesday evening**

We often fall into the trap of trying to recreate the experience of Sunday morning in our midweek small-group meeting. We forget that the dynamic of a handful of people is completely different from a congregation of a hundred or more (if you've ever heard four people applauding at the end of a song, you'll know what I mean). We need to take a step back, in order to rethink what works in a small setting.

**What is worship?**

But first, if we're going to help lead others in worship, it's important for us to understand what worship is all about. Often I find that people are familiar with the forms and structure of worship, but don't actually understand what is at the heart of our worship to God.

Let me first say what it is not. It is not singing songs or hymns, or reading scriptures, or even raising our hands or dancing. These are all things that can be useful *tools* in our expression of worship, but they aren't at the core. That would be like saying that great works of art are all about paint! Of course, we need tools that will help us express our worship; but God looks at the heart.

It is also not just about meetings. We can become so fixated with 'congregational worship', and even 'small-group worship', that we begin to think that worship is something we 'do' once or twice a week! And yet the Bible tells us that worship is something that should infuse the whole of our daily lives: our work, our play, our family time, our relationships, our driving(!), everything we are engaged in.

We might coalesce these thoughts into two main strands:

- Worship is my heart's response to God – Father, Son and Holy Spirit. It involves recognizing and responding to his character by inward and outward expressions of thanksgiving, praise and adoration. This attitude of thankfulness and praise is not limited to Christian gatherings, but should overflow into every part of my life.
- Worship also means lining up my life in accordance with God's character and will. It involves an ongoing yielding of myself to him, a willingness to hear his corrective voice and, as a consequence, to be changed by the power of the Holy Spirit in my daily life.

**Strengths of a small group**

As Morgan and I have prepared this book, we've found that, rather than having a list of things we *can't* do – shouting for joy, dancing, lying prostrate on the floor – there are certain dynamics that bring a richness and depth to small-group worship, which couldn't work in the larger setting. Here are a few of them:

1 *A relaxed, informal atmosphere.* A group of friends chatting together in a front room is a great setting for worship. Remember Jesus' promise in Matthew 18:20: 'For where two or three come together in my name, there am I with them.' Encourage the three-way conversation, moving easily and naturally between talking to one another, and talking to the Lord.

2 *Specific thanks.* In a small group, our praise and thanksgiving can move from generalities into specifics. For the Israelites, particular incidents became a cause for worship: the Passover, the parting of the Red Sea, entry into the Promised Land, and so on. It can be the same for

a small group: an answer to prayer, a new job, an opportunity to share the gospel. Our worship then becomes grounded in the reality of God's goodness to us in everyday life.

3   *All can participate.* In a small setting, everyone counts. Paul's statement in 1 Corinthians 14:26 ('When you come together, *everyone* has a hymn, or a word of instruction, a revelation . . .') can actually happen. And note Paul's insistence: '[they] *must* be done for the strengthening of the church'. When everyone participates, everyone benefits.

4   *Honesty.* The small group affords the opportunity for people to be more honest and open in their worship. In the Psalms we see not only joy and contentment, but also confusion, disappointment, frustration – even anger. However, these are expressed in the context of the unchanging faithfulness and love of God ('yet I will praise him'). In the small group we can acknowledge negative situations and feelings, and learn how to give thanks in the midst of them, in a way that may not be appropriate in a larger gathering.

5   *Ministry to one another.* When a small group of people meet together regularly, relationships develop and trust is built up, enabling us to minister to one another. As we worship and yield ourselves to God, personal issues often come to the surface. In a small group, those issues can be prayed through and followed up more easily than in a congregation.

6   *Accountability.* Small groups also give an opportunity for ongoing accountability. God doesn't want us to be spiritual lone rangers; his plan is for us to be involved in each other's lives, helping to 'spur one another on toward love and good works' (Hebrews 10:24). Spiritual

accountability and responsibility is an important principle of church life.

## How to use this book

It's very important to understand how this book is to be used. Each idea is a springboard, if you like, to inspire your group to worship. But it's the response in people's hearts that counts, and it's only when people are spontaneously expressing their thanks and praise to God that a time of worship comes alive.

In other words, most of what happens in your worship time should be unscripted! If there are no spontaneous contributions from the group, it's unlikely that your people are really engaging with God in worship. Make it clear from the beginning that you want everyone who can to participate.

Therefore, use only as much or as little of each idea as is necessary to get your group worshipping. Don't feel duty-bound to work your way right through each chapter. And if the worship begins to take a different direction to the one you expected, let it happen. It's more important for people to worship than for you to get to the bottom of the page! If it begins to flag, or go in a direction you feel isn't helpful, use a scripture or another section to put things back on course. But then be prepared to take a back seat again and let your group find its own unique expression of worship to God.

You will notice throughout the book that sometimes I talk *about* God and what he has done, and then without warning I address him directly in prayer. Generally speaking, I would encourage this kind of seamless move from discussion to prayer to praise and back to discussion again. However, you must of course feel free to develop your own style of communication within your group.

Here are some thoughts on how the sections within each idea are meant to be used:

## Introduction

This introduces the idea, and helps to set the course for the time of worship. It's the one section that can be read verbatim, but feel free to paraphrase it as desired.

## Activity

The activities vary in style, but are designed to help explore the subject. We've tried to avoid a conventional teaching style, opting instead for either a discovery or an analogy approach, as this encourages people to think and explore things for themselves.

Some of the Activities may unearth unusual responses, as people discover things about God or themselves that they hadn't seen before. Don't be phased by it, but encourage individuals to express what they've discovered in worship to God.

Some of the practical ideas may meet with some initial resistance. That's usually because people aren't used to doing fun things in church meetings! My recommendation is to persevere. The more relaxed your group can be when they are together, the more uninhibited they will be in their worship.

## Thanksgiving

This section either summarizes the discoveries made in the Activity section, or provides a focus for people to express their praise. It is laid out in bullet points for easy reference. In a more vocal, confident group, the prayers of thanks and praise will flow naturally from the Activity, but this section provides a back-up if people need help in directing their thoughts. Again, avoid just reading them out, and only use as many as are necessary to get the contributions flowing.

*Key Scriptures*

Three or four Key Scriptures are written out in full, for your easy reference, together with a short comment. This comment may be an insight, or a response in the form of a prayer. Other scriptures are simply included as references.

Get different people to read the scriptures out. It's an easy way to have more people participating, and it breaks the monotony of the leader's voice.

Always encourage people to put into their own words how the verse speaks to them. Again, avoid simply reading them out one after another, but only introduce them at the appropriate moments when a fresh idea is needed.

*Songs*

In our congregations, music is probably the central feature of our worship. Singing is a great way to express yourself, and everyone can participate. In most situations music can and should be part of our small-group worship, too. But where there are groups with no musicians or confident singers, musical worship can be a struggle. With this in mind, we've not made the Songs section integral to each Idea.

Use as many or as few of the songs as you need. They can either be sung one after another, or interspersed between scriptures.

All the songs listed are contained in the *Songs of Fellowship for Small Groups* songbook, which is available as both a words edition and as an easy-play music edition for musicians. Where you have a guitarist or keyboard player, or even just a good singer, by all means use them.

But for those groups that are short of these resources, we have included all the songs on a series of CDs, also entitled *Songs of Fellowship for Small Groups*, available from your local Christian bookshop (see the advert at the back of the book for details). These recordings are specially recorded and chosen to fit the small-group setting, with a solo voice and a simple, non-intrusive accompaniment.

CDs are particularly useful for instantly skipping to different tracks. You can even pre-programme your own order of songs. A remote control would also be very useful in this setting.

### Quotes

Quotes are sometimes humorous, usually thought-provoking. They are a useful tool to kick things off, but they may also help in the middle of a time of worship when it's tough going.

It's important not to be afraid to 'break the atmosphere'. Worship can get very intense sometimes, with every eye closed and a heavy silence hanging over the group. Just because we begin to talk and look at one another, and even laugh with one another, doesn't mean we've scared God's presence away! Remember, we're seeking to encourage a three-way conversation. When everyone is relaxed and comfortable, you can begin to direct your speech back towards God again.

### Application

We noted earlier that becoming more Christlike is an important part of worship. This section helps to apply what we've learned.

How you implement this section depends on the level of friendship and trust within the group. People could respond to these challenges (1) in the group setting, (2) by splitting into groups of two or three, or (3) on their own afterwards. However, the small-group setting offers the opportunity for **accountability and mutual encouragement on a regular** basis, so look to follow up these challenges in some way from week to week.

## Practical tips

Keep the focus Godward. Worship can encompass a whole realm of activities, feelings and responses, including adoration, celebration, praise, thankfulness, confession and repentance, commitment, forgiveness, personal ministry, intercession, healing, etc. All these are valid and important, but every worship time should by definition include at some stage a focusing away from ourselves and towards God, and a consequent expression of praise and worship for who he is and what he's done. Worship is primarily about and for him, not us. Don't allow personal ministry or problems to dominate.

Encourage people to bring their Bibles, so they can look up and read the scriptures for themselves. It may also avoid having to hand this book round!

This style of worship doesn't so much require a worship leader as a facilitator. Try to ensure that everyone is involved, but avoid embarrassing people who, for example, might be shy, or who dislike having to read things out. And don't be afraid to redirect things if they are going awry.

Even though the ideas are laid out in an instant, easy-to-use format, it's still important to spend a little time in preparation beforehand. Become familiar with the Activities, Application, and a couple of the scriptures, so you have some idea what direction you may want to go. Ask God to show you what he wants to do, and what particular things you should emphasize. Above all, ask God to cause worship to rise up in the hearts of the people. Pray that the different sections will bring revelation to them, so they might worship in spirit and truth.

Remember, the purpose is to spark people into spontaneous worship. This book is the touchpaper, not the firework. (But please don't set fire to it!) So although each idea only takes about five or ten minutes to read, with songs and spontaneous contributions, the worship time will be significantly longer. Be sensitive to the other elements that are important to the meeting, and don't squeeze them out without the agreement of the group leader.

Keep a diary of any specific challenges or prophetic words you feel God gives you as a group. God speaks to us far more than we realize, and so often we let those things go by without following them up or building them into our lives. Some may be for the group as a whole, and some may be for individuals. But they still need following up. Remember, the small group is an ideal context for mutual accountability and growth.

Above all, have fun. Being in God's presence is the most wonderful place anyone could ever be, and the small group is a uniquely powerful, intimate context in which to experience him.

May all your fireworks be spectacular!

*Stuart Townend*


NOTE: The observant among you will have noticed that I have made no reference to the use of spiritual gifts – tongues, prophecy, words of knowledge, gifts of healing – in worship.

I strongly believe in spiritual gifts, and would argue that the small group is the ideal setting for gifts to operate. However, I am aware of a wide range of views on the subject, and a very wide range of practices within the church as a whole. It's beyond the scope of this book to give specific guidelines on their use; the questions of how gifts are

expressed, when they should be used, and how they are dis-
cerned would probably fill a book on their own!

Suffice to say, where there is an understanding and prac-
tice of the gifts in the main meeting of your church, the use
of gifts in the small group should be strongly encouraged.
Give space for people to step out in using the gifts, and give
all the encouragement you can. We all have to start somewhere.

*Part 1: God the Father*

# 1. God Our Father 1

## INTRODUCTION

One of the most amazing results of being born again is coming into God's own family. We now have a heavenly Father unlike any father we could ever have on earth.

Understanding and receiving the fatherhood of God is central to our security and freedom in this life. When we know we are loved completely, lavishly and unconditionally, and we see ourselves as God sees us, that security enables us to love others in the same way.

Let's spend time considering the qualities of the Father who came to seek and save us, so that we could be embraced into his family.

## ACTIVITY

You will need a piece of paper and something to write with.

Jesus used an incredibly powerful story to demonstrate God's father heart towards us. The story of the prodigal son could just as readily be called the story of the loving father. Read out the parable in Luke 15:11–32 (it's particularly poignant in the *Message* translation), then as a group note down the characteristics of both the son and the father like this:

| *The son* | *but the father* |
|-----------|------------------|
| Was greedy | was generous to him |
| Was rebellious | was willing to let him go, etc. |

When you've finished, read out the list, but this time change 'the son' to 'I', and 'the father' to 'God'. Then begin to give thanks for his perfect fatherhood of each one of us.

## THANKSGIVING

- Your fathering love is perfect, even though we have sinned and rebelled against you. You don't lose your temper, or distance yourself from us. You welcome us with open arms, and lavish us with good things.
- You have placed each one of us in your family.
- You are the perfect father, daily providing for us, listening to us, speaking words of direction, comfort and encouragement, and correcting us when we go astray.

## KEY SCRIPTURES

1 John 3:1

*How great is the love the Father has lavished on us, that we should be called children of God! And that is what we are!*

Rebels and enemies of God, turned into loved, accepted children in his great family!

Ephesians 1:5

*[God] predestined us to be adopted as his sons through Jesus Christ, in accordance with his pleasure and will.*

We are adopted – in other words, he *chose* us to be his sons and daughters. We are handpicked children of God!

Isaiah 64:8

*Yet, O Lord, you are our Father.*
*We are the clay, you are the potter;*
*we are all the work of your hand.*

You are committed to shaping us and moulding us into the image of Jesus. But you don't change us in order to make us acceptable to you. It's the work of a loving Father who trains his children in the ways of righteousness.

Hebrews 12:10

*Our fathers disciplined us for a little while as they thought best; but God disciplines us for our good, that we may share in his holiness.*

Lord, even your discipline is the best thing that could happen to us. Even though it can be painful, we know it is from your loving hand, and that it is making us more like Jesus.

**See also**

Romans 8:15

SONGS (Disc 1)

1. Abba Father
2. I have heard (The Father's song)
3. I was lost without a trace (Like a child)
4. Father God I wonder (*Instrumental*)

## PRAYER

How can we ever put into words how wonderful it is to be in your family! Your care for us is constant and unconditional, and we look forward to knowing and being loved by you as a Father for ever. Amen.

## APPLICATION

How does the picture of God we have painted here shape the fathering of our own children? How accepting are we of them, irrespective of their behaviour? Do we love them enough to take time to correct them and train them lovingly in righteousness?

Encourage fathers in the group to look to this as a basis for their relationship with their own children.

Also, we must remember that 'fathering' or 'parenting' is a role we can play in other people's lives whether or not we are natural fathers (see, for example, Paul's reference to spiritual fathering in 1 Corinthians 4:15). Are there individuals for whom we should be a spiritual father, following the example of God's perfect fatherhood?

# 2. God Our Father 2

## INTRODUCTION

God didn't stop at salvation. He didn't just want to rescue us from sin, hell and eternal damnation – he wanted us in his own family. He wanted to be our Dad, and for us to be his children. That's why he chose us before the world was made. That's what drove Jesus to the cross. That's why he sent the Holy Spirit into our hearts, our seal of adoption. Let's take a moment to take in the wonder of it, and worship him.

## ACTIVITY

You will need two smallish pieces of paper for each member of the group, and something for each person to write with.

Start by giving the group three or four minutes to list on one piece of paper all the good things God our Father is like, e.g. caring, protective, plan-maker, strong, etc. When everyone has finished, encourage them to share what they have written with the group. Ask them to put the pieces of paper some-where safe (perhaps tucked inside their Bibles) to look at again another time.

Then ask the group to write on the second piece of paper the bad things that God our Father is not: impatient, overbearing, aggressive, distant, etc. Talk about these lists, too, but then ceremoniously rip them up and bin the rubbish.

Spend some time thanking God for what he is like.


## THANKSGIVING

- You provide everything we need.
- You love us unconditionally. No matter where I go or what I do, your father heart will not change towards me.
- You protect us.
- You are gentle with us.
- You're always there.
- You show no favouritism. The top executive and the poorest factory worker, the president and the refugee, all can know your fatherhood.


## KEY SCRIPTURES

Matthew 7:11

*If you, then, though you are evil, know how to give good gifts to your children, how much more will your Father in heaven give good gifts to those who ask him!*

Lord, you love to give good things to us, and you know what we need; in other words, you give with generosity *and* wisdom! You truly are the perfect father!

Galatians 4:6–7

*Because you are sons, God sent the Spirit of his Son into our hearts, the Spirit who calls out, 'Abba, Father.' So you are no longer a slave, but a son; and since you are a son, God has made you also an heir.*

This is more than an intellectual understanding of fatherhood. The indwelling of the Holy Spirit effects in us a profound change, and by that same Spirit we now experience the instinctive reaction of a child who longs to be with his own flesh and blood. We are now, by the Spirit as well as by law, children of God.

Psalm 68:5

*A father to the fatherless, a defender of widows, is God in his holy dwelling.*

God didn't choose to father the respectable son, the kind of son a dad could easily be proud of. He chose to father those who needed fathering – the weak, the foolish, those who had nothing to offer except themselves. He chose to father us.

SONGS (Disc 1)

5. I'm accepted
6. Let us draw near to God
7. O Father of the fatherless (Father me)
8. I love You, Lord (*Instrumental*)

PRAYER

Thank you, Lord, that you are our perfect Father. It gives us complete security to know your face is constantly turned towards us, and you will always love us more than we can know. You give without favouritism, and you give with immeasurable generosity. Yet you know what is good for us, and what isn't.

Lord, we put our trust in your fatherhood. We come to you in simple, childlike trust, placing our lives in your hands, and asking you for the power to grasp how immeasurably high and wide is your father love towards us. Amen.

## APPLICATION

Consider Ephesians 3:14–15:

*For this reason I kneel before the Father, from whom his whole family in heaven and on earth derives its name.*

It is not uncommon to hear people say: 'I can't relate to God as Father, because of my bad experiences with my own earthly father.' Our view of fatherhood is inevitably affected by our experience with our human fathers: whether positive, helping us to appreciate and feel God's fathering love; or negative, shaped by emotional or physical absence, rejection, or abuse.

But this scripture clearly demonstrates that God is the original, perfect father; *he* is the model for understanding fatherhood, not our own experiences. Now some people may need to go through a process of counselling and prayer regarding their past; there may be deep scars resulting from terrible past experience. But we need to see that, irrespective of the quality of our own earthly fathers, no one need be robbed of the security and pleasure of being loved by Father God.

# 3. God of Creation – Maker of the Heavens

## INTRODUCTION

It's obvious from the Psalms that people looking up into the skies were as awestruck by what they saw then as we are now. Of course, we know much more about the sun, the moon and the stars now than they did then. But it's fascinating that this knowledge, far from lessening our sense of wonder and amazement, only serves to increase it!

Let's 'consider the heavens' together, using what we know now to enhance our appreciation of the greatness and glory of God.

## ACTIVITY/KEY SCRIPTURES

Begin by considering Psalm 19:1–4 together. If you all have the same Bible translation, try reading it out loud together. If not, take a verse each.

*The heavens declare the glory of God;*
*    the skies proclaim the work of his hands.*
*Day after day they pour forth speech;*
*    night after night they display knowledge.*
*There is no speech or language*
*    where their voice is not heard.*
*Their voice goes out into all the earth,*
*    their words to the ends of the world.*

What an amazing statement! Not only are the heavens to be marvelled at; they are actually speaking to every one of us, telling us of the glory and majesty of God, every moment of every day. Let's take a moment to see what we can learn.

Find an encyclopedia or a book on astronomy (preferably with pictures) and read out some of the amazing facts about the universe – or you can use the ones below. Intersperse them with scriptures, as shown, and encourage people to respond in prayerful thanks.

1   It is estimated that a total of 8,000 stars are visible to the naked eye from earth. However, the number of stars that make up our galaxy, the Milky Way, is estimated to be more like 100,000 million. The Milky Way is in turn only one of several hundred million such galaxies within the viewing range of a large modern telescope – and those are only the ones we know about.

Psalm 147:4

*He determines the number of the stars*
*and calls them each by name.*

2   After the sun, the nearest star to our solar system is about 25 trillion miles from earth. The light from this star takes more than four years and three months to get to earth. A car travelling at 90 kilometres (50 miles) per hour would take 50 million years to get there!

Psalm 103:11

*For as high as the heavens are above the earth,*
*so great is his love for those who fear him.*

Nehemiah 9:6

*You alone are the Lord. You made the heavens, even the highest heavens, and all their starry host, the earth and all that is on it, the seas and all that is in them. You give life to everything, and the multitudes of heaven worship you.*

3   The sun is just one of the thousands of millions of stars that make up the Milky Way. To get some idea of scale, if you think of the Milky Way as being the size of the continent of Asia, our solar system is the size of a penny!

Psalm 8:3–5

*When I consider your heavens,*
  *the work of your fingers,*
*the moon and the stars,*
  *which you have set in place,*
*what is man that you are mindful of him,*
  *the son of man that you care for him?*
*You made him a little lower than the heavenly beings*
  *and crowned him with glory and honour.*

## THANKSGIVING

- Creation speaks of your limitless power – Jeremiah 32:17.
- Creation is a reflection of your own beauty – 2 Samuel 23:4.
- Creation belongs to you – Psalm 24:1.
- We can be sure that we are safe in your hands – Psalm 46:2.
- The One who commands creation also gives life and sustains it – Isaiah 42:5.

SONGS (Disc 1)

9. Who paints the skies?
10. Sing to the Lord (Awaken the dawn) (*Instrumental*)
11. All heaven declares
12. O Lord our God (We will magnify)

PRAYER

Lord, thank you for the wonder of your heavens. It reminds us of the extent of your power, your beauty, your rule, and your care. Yet our ultimate delight is not in appreciating your creation, but in knowing you. We put our trust in your unfailing love. Amen.

APPLICATION

Consider this quote:

> When God created the Creation, he made something where before there had been nothing, and as the author of the Book of Job puts it, 'the morning stars sang together, and all the sons of God shouted for joy' at the sheer and shimmering novelty of the thing . . .
>
> Using the same old materials of earth, air, fire and water, every 24 hours God creates something new out of them. If you think you're seeing the same old show all over again seven times a week, you're crazy. Every morning you wake up to something that in all eternity never was before and never will be again. And the you that wakes up was never the same before and will never be the same again either.
>
> Frederick Buechner, *Wishful Thinking* (Harper & Row, 1973)

Encourage people to consider how we might better appreciate God's amazing daily creativity in and around us.

# 4. God of Creation – Maker of the Earth

## INTRODUCTION

When people claim they can't see any evidence for the existence of God, they obviously aren't really looking! The
wonder of creation all points to a vast, powerful, bountiful,
extravagant God who cares for what he has made. Let's take
a moment to consider the glory of his handiwork, and give
him praise.

## ACTIVITY/KEY SCRIPTURES

Beforehand, gather together things that show the glory of
God's creation of earth: books on wildlife or nature, picture
calendars, a photograph of the world from space.
Alternatively, if you can plan ahead, video a wildlife pro-
gramme and watch a section of it. Encourage people to
comment on the things they notice.

Concentrate people's minds on the wonder of God's
*design*: these aren't accidents, the result of nature blindly
stumbling along; they, like us, are wonderfully put together,
displaying the Creator's imagination and ingenuity. You may
want to gather some amazing facts, like the ones below.

Begin to thank God for his acts of creation.

**Facts**

Scientists have made enormous progress in cataloguing the huge variety of animal and plant life on the earth. However, biologists estimate that somewhere between 500,000 and 5 million marine species have yet to be discovered and described.

Most of these live at the bottom of the deepest oceans, which are so deep that Mount Everest would be totally submerged in them!

Nehemiah 9:6

*You alone are the Lord. You made the heavens, even the highest heavens, and all their starry host, the earth and all that is on it, the seas and all that is in them. You give life to everything, and the multitudes of heaven worship you.*

When you break matter down into smaller and smaller pieces, you eventually come to the atom. Atoms are so small that 6 million of them would fit on the full stop at the end of this sentence. However, an atom is now believed to be composed of a dense nucleus containing protons and neutrons, surrounded by electrons orbiting in various layers. If the atom were the size of a football stadium then the nucleus would be a pea placed in the centre of the pitch!

But that's not all. Scientists have now been able to split even subatomic particles (i.e. protons, neutrons and electrons). These appear to be made of packets of energy – electromagnetic radiation – of which light is the visible component we are familiar with.

So when God said 'Let there be light' he really was creating the energy by which all matter is made.

Genesis 1:3–4

*And God said, 'Let there be light,' and there was light. God saw that the light was good, and he separated the light from the darkness.*

Many people aren't too excited about spiders. But there are a lot of them around! It is estimated that in autumn, a typical hectare of rough grassland will contain 5.5 million spiders!

Also, spider silk is the strongest fabric on the planet; it is even stronger than an equal diameter thread of steel.

In the face of danger, many lizards shed their tails. Special muscles cause the tail to wriggle to distract the predator, while the rest of the animal makes its escape. The lizards can regrow their tail after each shedding.

The Pallas's grass snake, a legless lizard, can 'shatter' its tail at all the joints. Each piece can wriggle on its own.

Psalm 24:1

*The earth is the Lord's, and everything in it,*
   *the world, and all who live in it.*

**To read together – Psalm 148**

If you all have the same version of the Bible, read it out together. If not, take a section each.

SONGS (Disc 1)

13. Our God is great
14. Your love, O Lord
15. My Jesus, my Saviour (Shout to the Lord)
16. Hills of the north rejoice (*Instrumental*)

## OTHER SCRIPTURES

1 Chronicles 16:30

*Tremble before him, all the earth!*
*    The world is firmly established; it cannot be moved.*

God holds the earth in his hands.

2 Samuel 23:4

*He is like the light of morning at sunrise*
*    on a cloudless morning,*
*like the brightness after rain*
*    that brings the grass from the earth.*

God's beauty is reflected in his creation.

## PRAYER

Lord, thank you for the wonder of your creation. We are surrounded by beauty, majesty, intricacy and ingenuity, and we worship you for the sheer extravagance of it all. Thank you that you are the same with us, lavishing grace and love upon us, attending to every detail of our lives, and demonstrating your unsurpassed power in and through us. We delight in being the apple of your eye. Amen.

## APPLICATION

How often do we stop to appreciate what God has made? In the coming week, try to find a time each day to stop your activity, and praise him for the splendour of his creation.

# 5. God of Creation – Maker of the Human Race

## INTRODUCTION

It's inspiring to view the creation around us, and marvel at the glory and creativity of God. But we tend to be less excited and awestruck about the pinnacle of God's creation – us! Perhaps we are too quick to focus on our faults and weaknesses. Perhaps the effects of sin and the Fall are painfully evident to us. But remember this: God viewed everything else he had made, and called it 'good'; but when he had made humans, he called it 'very good'. Let's consider the wonder of the way we are made, and praise God for his marvellous work.

## ACTIVITY/KEY SCRIPTURES

Find out some amazing facts about the human body – its complexity, its regenerative power, its resilience, etc. – and use them to point to God's creativity and care. Below are a few examples you can use. Intersperse the facts with scriptures, as shown below, and encourage people to respond in prayerful thanks.

**Facts**

The human body makes about 2 million red blood cells every second. When we are at rest, it takes the heart about one minute to pump all 5–7 litres (10–15 pints) of our blood through the body. That is no mean feat. Within each adult person is a vast, highly intricate system of arteries, veins and capillaries which total about 150,000 km (90,000 miles) in length!

Job 33:4

*The Spirit of God has made me;*
  *the breath of the Almighty gives me life.*

The brain is an incredibly complex mechanism. The average adult brain weighs only 1.4 kilograms (3 lb), yet it is made up of about 100,000 million nerve cells – and each one is esti-mated to be connected to 10,000 others.

Isaiah 64:8

*Yet, O Lord, you are our Father.*
  *We are the clay, you are the potter,*
  *we are all the work of your hand.*

The average adult's lungs contain about 2,400 kilometres (1,500 miles) of airways, with a total surface area of 360 square metres (430 square yards). There are 300 million alveoli (tiny air sacs at the end of the tubes) in each of your lungs; spread out flat, they would cover an area the size of a tennis court.

Genesis 2:7

*The Lord God formed the man from the dust of the ground and breathed into his nostrils the breath of life, and the man became a living being.*

Your breathing rate slows down from about 18 times a minute when you are awake, to 12 times a minute when you are asleep. Altogether, you will take about 600 million breaths during your lifetime.

Isaiah 42:5

*. . . [God the Lord] who created the heavens and stretched them out,*
   *who spread out the earth and all that comes out of it,*
   *who gives breath to its people,*
   *and life to those who walk on it.*

From conception, the development of the foetus in the womb follows the following pattern:

   0–4 weeks – the baby's heart develops and begins to beat.
   4–8 weeks – there are early movements, but these are not yet felt by the mother.
   8–12 weeks – the baby begins to suck and swallow. The kidneys begin to function, and pass urine from ten weeks. Foetal circulation now functions properly.
   16–20 weeks – fingernails develop. Toenails develop from 18 weeks.
   20–24 weeks – the baby responds to sounds and has periods of sleep and activity.

24–28 weeks – eyelids open, and there are respiratory movements.

32–36 weeks – the increased fat makes the body more rounded.

Psalm 139:13–16

*For you created my inmost being;*
*  you knit me together in my mother's womb.*
*I praise you because I am fearfully and wonderfully made;*
*  your works are wonderful,*
*  I know that full well.*
*My frame was not hidden from you*
*  when I was made in the secret place.*
*When I was woven together in the depths of the earth,*
*  your eyes saw my unformed body.*
*All the days ordained for me*
*  were written in your book*
*  before one of them came to be.*

Matthew 10:29–31

*Are not two sparrows sold for a penny? Yet not one of them will fall to the ground apart from the will of your Father. And even the very hairs of your head are all numbered. So don't be afraid; you are worth more than many sparrows.*

## THANKSGIVING

* The complexity of our bodies is a testimony to your glorious power.
* We are made in your image, able to think, feel and create like you.

- You have made us able to enjoy relationship with you, our Creator.
- You formed our bodies, and you sustain them. We need not fear for our physical or emotional health; instead we look to the One who numbers our days.

SONGS (Disc 1)

17. Far and near
18. Lord, how majestic You are
19. This is my desire (Lord, I give You my heart)
20. Woven together (Psalm 139)

PRAYER

We are awed by the way we are made. It is just another reminder of your creativity, your care and your love. And yet one day this body will return to dust, and we will be given new – even more amazing! – bodies at the resurrection.

APPLICATION

Consider 1 Corinthians 6:20:

*You were bought at a price. Therefore honour God with your body.*

We should not be fearful or worried about our physical health and well-being, because our lives are in God's hands. However, just as God gives us responsibility over the whole of creation, we have a responsibility to look after our own bodies.

Today, Christians in the West tend to be hard on some

things, and soft on others. For example, smoking and alcohol abuse get a hard time, but gluttony and laziness are overlooked.

Do we treat our bodies with respect? Are there ways we should adapt our lifestyle to come into line with this scripture?

# 6. God of Creation – the Wonder of the Familiar

## INTRODUCTION

When we think of creation, we tend to focus on the vastness of the heavens, or the power of nature reflecting God's own greatness. But we can also see God and learn more about him in the less spectacular, familiar things around us.

## ACTIVITY

Read Romans 1:20:

*For since the creation of the world God's invisible qualities – his eternal power and divine nature – have been clearly seen, being understood from what has been made, so that men are without excuse.*

This is an amazing verse: we cannot see God, but he has made his character and power clearly visible to every man and woman through what he has made. One of the places to see God, then, is in his creation!

Ask the members of the group to go outside for no more than three minutes, and find something connected with nature. When they return, ask each person to describe in detail what they have found. Some of the items, although simple and commonplace, may stimulate wonder and the beginnings of worship, which can then be continued through prayer and song.

The most conventional place to do this is in a garden. But there are still things to observe in a city street – the electricity that powers streetlights, animals, the rain, various sounds and sights, textures, etc.

Encourage people to look with fresh eyes, and appreciate God's creativity, his attention to detail, the freshness of colours and textures, the miracle of growth, and so on. Do these things tell us anything about the character of God?

Jesus didn't use religious objects or language to point to God. He used ordinary, everyday things that were part of the world of his hearers. Doors, gates, sheep, bread, lilies, birds – they all played a part in demonstrating God's character, his love, and his plan of salvation. We can use our observations as a basis for worshipping the One who created all things for his, and our, good pleasure.

## THANKSGIVING

- You provide us with everything we need.
- The wonder of creation reflects your wonderful character.
- You are constantly sustaining all the things around us – they only hold together because of your power.

## KEY SCRIPTURES

Matthew 6:28–30

*And why do you worry about clothes? See how the lilies of the field grow. They do not labour or spin. Yet I tell you that not even Solomon in all his splendour was dressed like one of these.*

The extravagance of your creation is often displayed in the little things. Before such a display of beauty and wonder, why should we worry about having what we need?

Psalm 19:1–4

*The heavens declare the glory of God;*
  *the skies proclaim the work of his hands.*
*Day after day they pour forth speech;*
  *night after night they display knowledge.*

Your creation speaks of you – constantly, loudly and clearly!

2 Samuel 23:4

*He is like the light of morning at sunrise*
  *on a cloudless morning,*
*like the brightness after rain*
  *that brings the grass from the earth.*

It's familiar enough: the sun rises every morning, and the rain falls regularly – perhaps too regularly for some. But every time we stop to look at it, it comes as a fresh, glorious experience. And that's true of our relationship with you. Each time we open our hearts in worship, we are renewed, and we see a little more of your glory.

SONGS (Disc 2)

1. Let everything that has breath
2. Over all the earth (Lord, reign in me)
3. Like the sunshine
4. All creatures of our God and King (*Instrumental*)

## PRAYER

Lord, we are only beginning to appreciate how amazing you are. Everything we see is a testimony to your glory. It reminds us of your provision to us, of your power to create and sustain, and of your sheer extravagance. Teach us not to take for granted your familiar gifts to us, but to stop regularly and respond in worship. Amen.

## APPLICATION

As we have seen, Jesus went out of his way to use familiar objects and ideas to point people to the spiritual reality of God. If Jesus were walking this earth now in twenty-first-century Britain, it would be reasonable to assume that he would not be talking about shepherds, seed-sowers and vineyards, but rubbish collectors, businessmen and gardens!

As we share the gospel with those we know, how can we use familiar images and experiences to point to the reality of God? Ask God for inspiration to communicate the gospel relevantly to unbelievers.

# 7. God the Provider

## INTRODUCTION

We tend to take it for granted, but God is the great Provider of all things. Not only did he design everything in creation for our needs and pleasure, but he is continually renewing it by his power. Neither we nor anything else in creation could exist without his constant, generous provision. Let us praise the One from whom all good things come.

## ACTIVITY

**Either:**

You will need a piece of paper and pen for each member of the group.

Ask everyone to make a written list of everything they have bought or have been given in the last 24 hours (not necessarily the whole contents of a supermarket trolley). Then ask each person to read some or all of their list. Thank God for his provision of your physical needs. Perhaps use Matthew 6:26–34 to help you focus on his promises and priorities.

If there are any in the group with pressing financial needs, it may be an appropriate part of worship to rally the rest of the group to help meet that need. Discuss this beforehand with the group leader, and how this could be done sensitively.

**Or:**

Ask people to suggest things God supplies that are essential to our lives (drink, food, clothes, oxygen, family, friendship, love).

Then ask people to suggest things that are not essential, but are there just as a sign of God's extravagant giving (colours, the seasons, snowflakes that are all different from one another, a brand new dawn every day).

Encourage people to thank God for his overwhelming, extravagant provision.

## THANKSGIVING

- You know every need we have.
- You supply all things with abundance and extravagance.
- You care for our physical, emotional and spiritual needs.
- You didn't just set the world in motion; you are constantly sustaining and providing for what you have made.

## KEY SCRIPTURES

**God's provision for all he has made**

Matthew 6:26

*Look at the birds of the air; they do not sow or reap or store away in barns, and yet your heavenly Father feeds them. Are you not much more valuable than they?*

Although God wants us to be good stewards of what he has given us, how often does our worry over finances and possessions indicate a reliance on our own earning power rather than on God's provision?

Colossians 1:15–17

*He is the image of the invisible God, the firstborn over all creation. For by him all things were created: things in heaven and on earth, visible and invisible, whether thrones or powers or rulers or authorities; all things were created by him and for him. He is before all things, and in him all things hold together.*

He knows what we need because he made us, and he has complete power and control over every aspect of creation. How can we doubt his ability to provide for us?

## God's special provision for his people

2 Peter 1:3

*His divine power has given us everything we need for life and godliness through our knowledge of him who called us by his own glory and goodness.*

We're called to a life of godliness. However, we achieve it not by our own strength, but by drawing on God's provision of power within us. We have all we need, not just to survive, but to live victoriously.

Matthew 6:8

*Your Father knows what you need before you ask him.*

Lord, you understand our needs better than we do. We can rely on your judgement and goodness to give us what is best.

## See also

Matthew 6:33–34 – if we seek his kingdom and his righteousness, we can be free from worrying about our needs.

## SONGS (Disc 2)

5. Who is there like You?
6. Draw me close to You
7. The steadfast love of the Lord
8. We bow down

## PRAYER

Thank you for your daily provision, both for our needs and for our delights – you truly are an extravagant Father who gives his children the best! We are sorry that we take you so much for granted. Please help us to be continually thankful for all you give to us. Amen.

## APPLICATION

Sometimes we miss out on the wonder of his provision because we are too preoccupied with looking inward at our own problems. Sometimes we fail to receive his best, because we strive to provide for ourselves without looking to him.

Ask God to show you areas where you fail to look to him (financial provision, a future husband/wife, his protection of your family), then pray through them together as a group or in twos, asking God to change you.

# 8. God the Healer

## INTRODUCTION

One of the most dramatic features of Jesus' ministry on earth was his ministry of healing. It not only demonstrated God's power and substantiated Jesus' identity as the Son of God; it also demonstrated God's compassion for those in need, and his desire that people become whole.

Jesus' ministry goes on today. His body, the church, is called to do the works of Jesus, and the same Spirit that anointed him, anoints us today. Now, just as then, incidents of healing indicate that the kingdom of God is advancing.

## ACTIVITY

Ask people to share any instances where they (or someone they know well) have received some measure of healing, whether physical, emotional or spiritual. Has the healing been instant, or gradual? Did it happen as they were being prayed for, or some time later? Did they feel anything as they were being healed?

We should not be surprised that people's experiences vary. Even in the gospels, no two healings that Jesus did seem to have been the same. Some were gradual, others instant; some were immediate, others happened later; some involved touching, others didn't. At least one didn't involve prayer at all; another happened at several miles' distance, and one involved mud and spit applied to the eyes!

Jesus didn't just bring physical healing. His ministry left people saved, revitalized, on fire for God, repentant, restored, and loved.

Encourage each one to thank God for the specific healing that has taken place, and for the ongoing work of healing in our lives.

## THANKSGIVING

- You care about our physical, emotional and spiritual condition, and you are at work in us continually to bring wholeness.
- You gave our bodies natural healing qualities that are common to us all, but are remarkable nonetheless.
- You work in many and varied ways to bring about healing.
- You feel compassion when we are suffering.
- All your work in us brings about healing of one kind or another.
- Healing is the consequence of the atoning work of your Son Jesus on the cross.

## KEY SCRIPTURES

### Mark 1:40–42

*A man with leprosy came to him and begged him on his knees, 'If you are willing, you can make me clean.' Filled with compassion, Jesus reached out his hand and touched the man. 'I am willing,' he said. 'Be clean!' Immediately the leprosy left him and he was cured.*

Jesus was moved by suffering, just as we are. And he hasn't changed!

Psalm 103:2–3

*Praise the Lord, O my soul,*
*  and forget not all his benefits –*
*who forgives all your sins*
*  and heals all your diseases.*

God's healing and forgiving power is a cause for praise. Let's not forget any of the many and varied benefits that his forgiveness and healing bring.

Isaiah 53:5

*But he was pierced for our transgressions,*
*  he was crushed for our iniquities;*
*the punishment that brought us peace was upon him,*
*  and by his wounds we are healed.*

It's important to see that healing is part of the atonement. His suffering and death is the power by which we can be forgiven *and* healed.

James 5:14–16

*Is any one of you sick? He should call the elders of the church to pray over him and anoint him with oil in the name of the Lord. And the prayer offered in faith will make the sick person well; the Lord will raise him up. If he has sinned, he will be forgiven. Therefore confess your sins to each other and pray for each other so that you may be healed. The prayer of a righteous man is powerful and effective.*

God wants us to pray for one another. We can each be instruments in bringing healing and wholeness to one another – what a privilege!

## SONGS (Disc 2)

9. I believe in Jesus
10. Say the word
11. Anointing fall on me
12. I want to be out of my depth in Your love

## PRAYER

Lord, we praise you for your wonderful kindness to us. Thank you that the cross was not just about salvation and eternal life, but about wholeness, peace and joy. Even though that process of wholeness won't be fully realized in our lifetimes, we know that one day we will stand before you as new creations, without spot or blemish, whole and complete in you. Amen.

## APPLICATION

Are there any in the group who need God's healing touch right now? Pray with those who would like to be prayed with. And pray with faith, believing that God can and does heal.

IMPORTANT NOTE: When the subject of healing comes up in a group, it is not uncommon for people to be more taken up with the question of why God doesn't heal, than by the fact that he does! Don't allow the worship time to be sidetracked. Explain that this is an important question, and that if people want to explore it further, they (or you as a group) could look at some of the many excellent books on the subject. Right now you want to focus on the fact that God does heal, and that is shown by the stories that people are sharing of how God has touched them.

Some people tend to pray an 'if it be thy will' prayer. That's not really a 'prayer offered in faith' (James 5:15). Rather than praying in such a way as to keep our options open, we should be asking God in our own hearts how we should pray, and then praying in accordance with his leading and our faith.

# 9. God's Love

## INTRODUCTION

We're all familiar with the idea that God loves us. We're taught it through songs at Sunday school, through sermons at church, and in the Bible. But do we ever stop to consider the magnitude of this statement?

This is the God of the universe, the One who set trillions upon trillions of stars and planets in space, of which our own planet is the tiniest speck. This is the God of the earth, who exhibits such enormous power when lightning strikes, or the earth quakes, or a hurricane hits.

In fact, the love of God is *the* most powerful force in creation – stronger than earthquakes, brighter than the brightest star. The Bible makes it so central to the nature of God that at one point John simply says, 'God is love' (1 John 4:16).

This love caused galaxies to come into being, brought God himself to earth as a ransom, raised him from the dead, and now is extravagantly poured out on each one of us. What a cause for worshipping him!

## ACTIVITY

You will need:

1   Two A4 pieces of paper or card, each cut out into a heart shape and joined with sticky tape or glue, leaving an opening at the top, to form a heart-shaped 'wallet'.
2   Some smaller pieces of paper, one for each member of the group.
3   A red candle (optional).

Begin by considering the love of God using some of the scriptures and songs listed below. At an appropriate point ask each member of the group to write their name on a piece of paper and then put it into the heart. Seal the top of the heart to symbolize the permanence of God's love for us.

You could seal the heart using the red candle by dripping the melted wax onto the paper or card, symbolizing the blood of Christ – but do it with care; don't mess up someone's table, or set fire to the kitchen!

## THANKSGIVING

*   Your love is completely unconditional; I can never earn it, I can never lose it.
*   You don't just love the faceless mass of humanity. You love me!
*   Your love will hold me fast for ever, whatever the devil, the world, even my friends and family may do to me.
*   Your love is more powerful than my weakness.
*   Your love is more than words or feelings. It is clearly, tangibly demonstrated in the gift of Jesus.

## KEY SCRIPTURES

### Psalm 36:5–7

*Your love, O Lord, reaches to the heavens,*
*  your faithfulness to the skies . . .*
*  How priceless is your unfailing love!*

Of course, the skies have no limit! Your love for me is of infinite size, and of infinite value.

### Romans 8:38–39

*For I am convinced that neither death nor life, neither angels nor demons, neither the present nor the future, nor any powers, neither height nor depth, nor anything else in all creation, will be able to separate us from the love of God that is in Christ Jesus our Lord.*

When we feel rejected and unloved, when we feel attacked and isolated, we need to reject the lies, and remember the truth – God's love is ours for ever.

### Ephesians 3:17–19

*I pray that you, being rooted and established in love, may have power, together with all the saints, to grasp how wide and long and high and deep is the love of Christ, and to know this love that surpasses knowledge – that you may be filled to the measure of all the fulness of God.*

Amazing – we need God's power even to *understand* how great is the love of God, never mind experience it ourselves. And when we do begin to know it for ourselves, we begin to be filled with all the fullness of God himself! This is no intellectual process; this is a real, powerful, almost tangible encounter with God.

## 1 John 3:1

*How great is the love the Father has lavished on us, that we should be called children of God!*

God's love drove him not just to salvation, but to adoption. He could just have rescued us; instead, he brought us right into the heart of his family.

**See also**

1 John 4:10 – to understand what love is, we shouldn't look at ourselves, at the way we love or have been loved by others. We need to look at God's pure, giving, selfless love, demonstrated in Jesus.

Psalm 63:3 – God's love is better than life.

## SONGS (Disc 2)

13. How wonderful
14. Over the mountains and the sea (I could sing of Your love for ever)
15. I stand amazed
16. Such love

## PRAYER

Lord, your love is overwhelming; it's unconditional; it's limitless; it holds me secure and will be with me for ever, because my name is written on your heart. May I grow every day in my understanding and experience of this love, and so become more like Christ by loving those around me in the same way that you love me.

## APPLICATION

Ephesians 3 and Romans 5 suggest that we need the Holy Spirit's help to know the extent of God's love in a life-changing way. Sometimes we can resist the Spirit's work because of our self-image – we don't accept that God could love us. Let's pray with each other, and ask God for a powerful, fresh revelation of his love in our lives.

# 10. God's Protection

## INTRODUCTION

We are often reminded of how dangerous our society has become. Stories of burglaries, crimes of violence, road rage, child abuse, all regularly dominate our televisions and newspapers. But we can also feel vulnerable in other ways: to stress, to depression, to criticism and to rejection by others.

Our natural reaction to all these things might be to become more cautious, perhaps even more fearful. Our lives can become hemmed in by worry about what might happen to ourselves, our loved ones, and our possessions.

God doesn't want us to be fearful! The Bible clearly states again and again that God is our Protector, our Fortress and our Rock. His protection is expressed in several ways, as we shall see. But it all points to both his *ability* to protect us – as the omnipotent God – and his *willingness* to look after us – his nurturing care for his children. We can come to him in thanks and praise, confident in his complete commitment to us.

## ACTIVITY

As a group, meditate on Psalm 62. Explain that you are going to read out one verse at a time, and in the silence that follows, ask people to respond with a prayer or a comment.

It's a very practical psalm, so encourage people to be specific in their response.

Some of the key themes to try to bring out:

- 'God alone' (vv. 1, 2, 5, 6) – we should look to him alone for rest and protection.
- 'I will never be shaken' (vv. 2, 6) – it's a statement of faith and resolve, as well as a fact of God's protection. Encourage people to speak that out together.
- 'Pour out your hearts to him' (v. 8) – God's not angry that we are worried or fearful; but he wants us to unload it on to him.
- 'Don't trust in riches' (v. 10) – sometimes our fear comes from being possessive about things. We need to recognize that possessions come from God.

## THANKSGIVING

- You are King of kings, with all power and authority over everything that might seek to hurt us.
- You know our weaknesses, and your grace is sufficient.
- Your protection is constant and complete.

## KEY SCRIPTURES

Psalm 91:4

*He will cover you with his feathers,*
  *and under his wings you will find refuge;*
  *his faithfulness will be your shield and rampart.*

God's wings provide us with shade from the heat, and make us invisible to the enemy. They are also a place of comfort and intimacy. There is no better place to be!

John 10:28

*I give them eternal life, and they shall never perish; no-one can snatch them out of my hand.*

We are in Jesus' hand! The hand that set the stars in place, that healed the sick and raised the dead, that submitted to the agony of the cross, that now bears the scars of his sacrifice – that hand will hold us fast for ever.

Psalm 59:16

*But I will sing of your strength,*
*  in the morning I will sing of your love;*
*for you are my fortress,*
*  my refuge in times of trouble.*

God's protection causes us to rejoice in him; thanks and praise are an expression of our confidence in his power and commitment to us.

**See also**

Proverbs 14:26 – the promise is for us and our families.

Psalm 17:8 – we are the objects of his love, and we can find shade in his wings.

SONGS (Disc 2)

17.  Blessed be the name of the Lord
18.  Come to the Power
19.  You are my passion
20.  Your love looks after me

## ANOTHER ACTIVITY

As we have said, God's protection of us is not only physical. In what other ways do we find ourselves under attack and therefore needing protection?

- Verbal attack by enemies of the gospel.
- Spiritual attack from demonic forces.
- Emotional attack from depression, relationships.

How do we find God's protection and strength in each of these areas?

## PRAYER

Lord, we thank you for your constant, caring protection. We choose to put our trust in you, not ourselves. Thank you that you are shelter in the storm, refuge when we're attacked, shade in the heat of pressure, and a shield as we work to advance your kingdom. Amen.

## APPLICATION

God's supply is always sufficient. But we need to be wise in ordering our own lives. For example, going to bed late will make us tired, and tiredness can make us more susceptible to all sorts of attack.

What decisions do you need to make today to co-operate with God's protection in your life?

# 11. God's Presence

## INTRODUCTION

The heart of the Christian faith is not a set of beliefs, or a lifestyle, or even heaven when you die; it's a living relationship with a loving God. And by the power of the Holy Spirit we can know him and experience his presence right now.

## ACTIVITY

Ask people to share their experiences of God's presence, whether it was in a meeting, or by themselves. Ask if they can put into words how it felt: peaceful, warm, powerful, gentle? Emphasize that whether we feel anything or not, we can still enjoy his presence, but sometimes God encourages us by touching our bodies or our emotions.

We don't need an exciting meeting or special songs to know his presence. Encourage people to close their eyes, perhaps to lift their hands, and in the quiet enjoy God's presence in the room. Some might find it helpful to picture in their mind's eye Jesus standing in front of them, his arms outstretched to welcome them.

## THANKSGIVING

- You are always with us.
- We have access to you, not through pious living or religious ceremony, but through Jesus. Your blood is enough to bring us into your very throne-room!
- We can experience your presence not just in a service, but at home, in the car, at work, everywhere.
- Not only do we desire to fellowship with you, but you desire to fellowship with us.

## KEY SCRIPTURES

Psalm 27:4

*One thing I ask of the Lord,*
  *this is what I seek:*
*that I may dwell in the house of the Lord*
  *all the days of my life,*
*to gaze upon the beauty of the Lord*
  *and to seek him in his temple.*

Lord, we lay aside all other needs and desires, in order to seek one thing: to dwell with you, and to see your beauty. We desire only you. By your Holy Spirit, open our eyes to see you now.

Matthew 18:20

*For where two or three come together in my name, there am I with them.*

God promises to be present at even the most poorly attended meeting! God's not interested in numbers; he's interested in people who will welcome him.

Psalm 42:1–2

*As the deer pants for streams of water,*
*so my soul pants for you, O God.*
*My soul thirsts for God, for the living God.*
*When can I go and meet with God?*

This is a heartfelt, thirsty cry for your presence, Lord. Make us more hungry for you.

Psalm 139:7–10

*Where can I go from your Spirit?*
*Where can I flee from your presence?*
*If I go up to the heavens, you are there;*
*if I make my bed in the depths, you are there.*
*If I rise on the wings of the dawn,*
*if I settle on the far side of the sea,*
*even there your hand will guide me,*
*your right hand will hold me fast.*

This isn't the cry of a man desperate to escape God. It's the assurance of a man who knows that wherever we are, however high or low we might swing, from the heights of euphoria to the depths of despair and depression – he's not only there, he's holding us fast.

### See also

Matthew 28:19–20 – wherever we go for the sake of the gospel, no matter how difficult or isolating, the promise of Jesus is to be with us.

1 John 4:13 – how do we know that he is with us? Because his Spirit dwells inside us.

SONGS (Disc 3)

1. I will seek Your face
2. Be still, for the presence of the Lord
3. To be in Your presence
4. As the deer (*Instrumental*)

PRAYER

Lord, thank you for the gift of your presence. Thank you that it can't be earned, or worked up – it's the result of your promise, and of your gift of the Holy Spirit in every believer. Draw us again and again to be still and enjoy your wonderful presence in every aspect of our lives. Amen.

QUOTE

If God does not enter your kitchen, there is something wrong with your kitchen. If you can't take God into your recreation, there is something wrong with your play. We all believe in the God of the heroic. What we need most these days is the God of the humdrum, the commonplace, the everyday.

Peter Marshall, Sr

APPLICATION

We need to practise the presence of God. If God is always with us by his Spirit within us, we can know his presence in every situation. In what practical ways can we invite God in the coming week into the car, the home, the office or school – especially where there is pressure and difficulty?

Some people have posters, keyrings or wristbands to remind them of God's presence and promises. How do you remind yourself of God's constant presence?

# 12. God's Faithfulness

## INTRODUCTION

The faithfulness of God is a common theme in the Scriptures. It's so integral to his character that it is often twinned with his love. In fact, just as the Bible says that God *is* love, so it says that God *cannot* be unfaithful.

## ACTIVITY

What do we mean when we say God is faithful? Here are some other helpful words from a thesaurus that help us to grasp the wonder of God's faithfulness:

*Constant* – like the sun's rays, never failing, never weakening.
*Dependable* – like the fruitful earth, like day following night.
*Devoted* – like a close friend or husband/wife, who only does the best for you, who holds nothing back, who makes you feel *special*.
*Unswerving* – like an arrow, which won't be blown off course, but unerringly finds its mark.
*Unwavering* – like a mountain, like the earth beneath our feet, certain and solid.

**Either:**

Tell the group about someone you know whom you consider to be very faithful. Explain why you describe him or her as such. Ask others to do the same for people they know. Point out that we are made in the image of God, and the human faithfulness we experience in others is but a pale reflection of God's faithfulness. What we see and praise in our friends is even more praiseworthy in God.

**And/or:**

Ask people to share any examples they can think of where they could clearly see the faithfulness of God in a situation (e.g. in how they became a Christian, in protection for them or their family, in times of pressure or difficulty). Begin to encourage people to speak out their thanks to God.

## THANKSGIVING

- Your faithfulness is an unchangeable part of your character.
- You prove your faithfulness in good times and in bad.
- You are faithful in even the smallest detail.
- Your commitment to us is expressed supremely in the cross.
- Our imperfect faithfulness to one another is a pale shadow of your supreme, perfect faithfulness.

## KEY SCRIPTURES

Deuteronomy 32:4

*He is the Rock, his works are perfect,*
*and all his ways are just.*

*A faithful God who does no wrong,*
  *upright and just is he.*

Your faithfulness is sure. You don't promise anything you can't deliver. You are strong, perfect, faithful *and* just.

Lamentations 3:22–23

*Because of the Lord's great love we are not consumed,*
  *for his compassions never fail.*
  *They are new every morning;*
  *great is your faithfulness.*

Your faithfulness is demonstrated every day of our lives by your wonderful mercies to us. Every morning brings fresh provision and strength, fresh protection and wisdom to live a life of joy and godliness.

1 Corinthians 10:13

*No temptation has seized you except what is common to man. And God is faithful; he will not let you be tempted beyond what you can bear. But when you are tempted, he will also provide a way out so that you can stand up under it.*

We can depend on your faithfulness, even in times of trial. When the pressure is on, we need to remind ourselves that you are still faithful – this is not beyond your power or your control.

2 Timothy 2:13

*If we are faithless,*
  *he will remain faithful,*
  *for he cannot disown himself.*

It's part of your perfect character. We fail, yet you stay the same. You cannot be unfaithful!

**See also**

Revelation 19:11 – Jesus' very name is Faithful and True.

Psalm 85:10–11 – love, faithfulness, righteousness and peace.

SONGS (Disc 3)

5.  Great is Thy faithfulness
6.  Lord, I come before Your throne of grace
7.  Faithful One
8.  The day Thou gavest, Lord, is ended (*Instrumental*)

PRAYER

Thank you, Lord, that everything you do is right, and because of your faithfulness, everything you do is for our good. We look over our lives and see this demonstrated again and again, even when at the time we doubted you. We acknowledge that you are trustworthy in every situation of our lives. Help us to grow daily in our faith, so that we prove you even in difficulties and pressures. Amen.

## APPLICATION

As we have seen, God is faithful in everything, so there are no circumstances in which we cannot trust him. Share any situations that God brings to mind where you need to fix your eyes on him again. How will this affect your attitudes, words and actions?

# 13. God of Peace 1

## INTRODUCTION

We tend to think of peace today as the absence of something – of war, of noise, and so on. But the Bible's idea of peace (*shalom* in the Old Testament, *eirene* in the New) is of well-being and rest. Let's explore the wonder of the peace of God as we worship him together.

## ACTIVITY

Consider the following familiar scripture:

Psalm 46:10
*Be still, and know that I am God.*

Anyone who has young children knows that getting them to sit still so that you can communicate with them is a major task! That's because

- they are easily distracted;
- they have their own agendas;
- they are unaware of what should take priority;
- they often want to talk before having to listen.

Sound familiar? As God's children we are often the same. He has to make us still in order to communicate with us. How does God do this? (To help answer the question, you may want to consider the analogy of the parent–child relationship; how do we get through to our own kids?)

Remember, too, the story of Martha and Mary (Luke 10:38–42). How much do we rush about when it is better to sit and listen?

The Quakers grasped this concept. Instead of holding church meetings that were full of activity and 'things we can do for God', they sat in silence until someone felt they had a word from the Lord. The reason they were called Quakers was because God was so powerfully present at these meetings that they shook violently!

Take five minutes (or as long as you feel appropriate) to sit in silence together. Encourage people to shut their eyes, lay aside all distracting thoughts and issues, and just focus on him. Afterwards discuss together what it was like, and ask if anyone felt that God spoke to them. Then begin to worship the God of peace.

## THANKSGIVING

- You are always speaking to us, even when we are not listening.
- You bring rest, even in the midst of pressure and testing.
- Your peace is not dependent on circumstances, and it transcends human understanding.
- Receiving your peace turns us into men and women of peace, taking that peace wherever we go.

## KEY SCRIPTURES

### Proverbs 14:30

*A heart at peace gives life to the body,*
*but envy rots the bones.*

One aspect of peace is being content with what you have.

### Isaiah 26:3

*You will keep in perfect peace*
*him whose mind is steadfast,*
*because he trusts in you.*

It's important whom we focus on. When we listen to the devil's lies, or focus on the circumstances – as Peter did when walking on water – we cease to trust. We should ask the Lord for a steadfast mind that believes his promises.

### John 14:27

*Peace I leave with you; my peace I give you. I do not give to you as the world gives. Do not let your hearts be troubled and do not be afraid.*

God *gives* peace. We don't earn it. We don't logically arrive at it. We don't exert positive thinking. We receive it.

### Philippians 4:7

*And the peace of God, which transcends all understanding, will guard your hearts and your minds in Christ Jesus.*

If we let God's peace overwhelm us, it will provide protection for our hearts and minds. We will not be knocked off balance by a sudden turn of events, a hurtful comment, or greater pressure.

## SONGS (Disc 3)

9. Quiet my mind
10. I will wait
11. Father God, fill this place
12. Dear Lord and Father of mankind (*Instrumental*)

## QUOTES

The amazing thing about a man being arrested for disturbing the peace is that he actually found any.

From *14,000 Quips and Quotes* by E. C. McKenzie (Baker, 1980)

Rest is not a hallowed feeling that comes over us in church; it is the repose of a heart set deep in God.

Henry Drummond
quoted in *The Speaker's Sourcebook* (Zondervan, 1975)

## PRAYER

Thank you that your peace is life and fullness to us; that it can't be achieved or striven for – it can only be given and received. Teach us to stop in the midst of our activity, in order to hear your voice and receive your refreshing. And let your peace characterize every aspect of our lives: our words, our relationships, our activities, and our plans. May we be men and women of peace, shining as lights in a troubled world. Amen.

## APPLICATION

Remember the story of Jesus calming the storm (Mark 4:35–41)? Jesus speaks peace to the winds and the waves, and the disciples are amazed. We often interpret this passage to mean that Jesus calms the storms in our lives. But in fact Jesus rebukes the disciples for their fear and lack of faith. In other words, the situation was never out of control; they were never in danger (note in verse 35 that Jesus had said *they were going to the other side*, not to the bottom of the lake).

Are worry and fear robbing you of your peace? Are you expecting God to calm the storm, when in fact he wants you to trust him in it? Confess your worries to him this week, declare his sovereignty in every situation, and ask for his peace to invade your mind and emotions.

# 14. God of Peace 2

## INTRODUCTION

When we look at the world we are hard-pushed to find peace anywhere. Even in places where there are no wars or civil disturbances, there seems to be political in-fighting, worries about the economy, racial tension, fears about an increasingly violent society, arguments about education, employment . . . and the list goes on. Peace and contentment seem to be rare qualities indeed.

Some consider Christianity a refuge from the storm of life; a place of retreat to stained-glass windows, Bach fugues and comforting platitudes for an hour a week. But the peace that God gives is something very different.

## ACTIVITY

Consider these two rather unusual verses on the subject of peace:

Isaiah 9:6–7

*And he will be called*
*Wonderful Counsellor, Mighty God,*
*Everlasting Father, Prince of Peace.*
*Of the increase of his government and peace*
*there will be no end.*

Colossians 3:15

*Let the peace of Christ rule in your hearts, since as members of one body you were called to peace. And be thankful.*

You may have heard of the Pax Romana (Roman Peace). It was a period achieved in regions where the Roman Empire had subdued the 'barbarian' locals, managing to bring about an end to hostilities and establish a new government and system of law. It was an expansion of Roman government and a spread of Roman culture which completely changed the way people in conquered territories lived. Obviously, the Pax was more stable in some places than in others, but where it worked, it actually benefited local people socially – as long as the regional administrators weren't corrupt!

God's peace is like that. A powerful, invading force but which only works when the people stop resisting and accept that another power is now in charge – a Prince, no less.

Are we resisting this Prince of Peace in any way, still wanting to govern our own affairs? Or are we accepting that another Power wants to increase his government and peace in every sphere of our lives?

Let's worship and acknowledge the Prince of Peace.

## THANKSGIVING

- Your peace is an active, powerful force at work in our lives as we yield to you.
- You bring peace even to the toughest situation.
- We can be instruments of peace to others.

## KEY SCRIPTURES

### Psalm 119:165

*Great peace have they who love your law,*
  *and nothing can make them stumble.*

When we delight to follow your ways, your peace makes us
sure-footed, even in extreme stress and pressure.

### Isaiah 32:17

*The fruit of righteousness will be peace;*
  *the effect of righteousness will be quietness and confidence*
*for ever.*

There is enormous power in doing the right thing. Not only
will we be at peace with ourselves, but it will extend God's
rule of peace into the situation.

### Ephesians 2:14–15

*For he himself is our peace, who has made the two [Jews and*
*Gentiles] one and has destroyed the barrier, the dividing wall*
*of hostility, by abolishing in his flesh the law with its com-*
*mandments and regulations.*

You have broken down the barriers that divided people,
enabling all to come to you, not by works or accident of
birth, but by your blood and by faith in you alone.

SONGS (Disc 3)

13. O righteous God
14. He is our peace
15. Make me a channel of Your peace
16. Your name is peace

## QUOTE

Christmas carol singers sing about peace on earth but they don't tell us where.

From *14,000 Quips and Quotes* by E. C. McKenzie (Baker, 1980)

## PRAYER

Thank you for the power of your peace. Thank you that it can reign in our lives, that it is constantly on the increase as your kingdom grows. May we know what it means to have peace reigning in every situation of our lives, and help to extend your reign of peace to those around us. Amen.

## APPLICATION

What circumstances of our lives need the powerful peace of God to break in right now? It might be our home, family, work, school, a particular relationship. Break into twos and pray for peace to reign in those situations.

# 15. The Holiness of God

## INTRODUCTION

A scriptural understanding of holiness involves two elements: one is a separation from any kind of evil or sin; and the second is a total dedication and devotion to the Lord and his glory. We are often tempted to think of personal holiness as obeying a list of 'do nots'; but it has far more to do with passion, commitment, and a desire to serve him in everything.

God's holiness is like that: his absolute purity is completely separate from any trace of evil or sin; but it's also a purity of passion, a purity of love, a purity of joy that is so intense and glorious that it bathes him in unapproachable light (1 Timothy 6:16).

Unapproachable . . . yet we may approach. Who can stand in his presence (1 Samuel 6:20)? . . . yet we may stand before him, because of the blood of his Son. Let's boldly approach the throne of grace and worship the Holy One with reverence, awe and love.

## ACTIVITY

Slowly read out the whole of Revelation 4. Get people to close their eyes and imagine they are there, seeing the sights and hearing the sounds as the scene is being described. With eyes still closed, ask people to put into words what they see and feel. (For some it might be awesome, noisy, terrifying, glorious.)

Remind them that this is the activity of heaven right now, and as we worship in this small group, we are actually joining with the elders, the living creatures, and the thousands upon thousands of angels giving glory to the Lamb who was slain.

## THANKSGIVING

- You are glorious, clothed in majesty and holiness, bathed in splendour and light.
- You are the same One who walked this earth in humility, demonstrating your love for sinners by giving your life as a sacrifice.
- Now by your blood, you welcome us into your glorious presence.
- We are holy, because you are holy – we are 'in Christ'.

## KEY SCRIPTURES

Exodus 15:11

*Who among the gods is like you, O Lord?*
*Who is like you –*
　*majestic in holiness,*
　*awesome in glory,*
　*working wonders?*

Thank you, Lord, that no one can match your greatness. No power can threaten your sovereign rule. And no one can compare with you for tenderness, love and faithfulness.

Hebrews 10:22

*Let us draw near to God with a sincere heart in full assurance of faith, having our hearts sprinkled to cleanse us from a guilty conscience and having our bodies washed with pure water.*

We can draw near to you with confidence, not fear. You are the holy God, but your cleansing of us is complete and for ever.

Colossians 3:12

*Therefore, as God's chosen people, holy and dearly loved, clothe yourselves with compassion, kindness, humility, gentleness and patience.*

We do not clothe ourselves with these qualities in order to be holy. We do it because we are already holy, made clean by Jesus' blood, not by anything we have done.

SONGS (Disc 3)

17. Behold the Lord
18. Holy, holy (Lift up His name)
19. This is the place (Holy ground)
20. Purify my heart (Refiner's fire)

PRAYER

Lord, you are the Holy One, the supreme King of heaven and earth. Your name makes the demons tremble, yet it is music to our ears. Let your glory fill our gaze more and more.

We lay our lives before you, as a holy sacrifice. Our righteousness is as filthy rags, but we are clothed in your righteousness, and we enter your holy presence with confidence, knowing we are accepted and loved by you. Amen.


## APPLICATION

After St Augustine became a Christian, he still often passed a drinking place where he had previously been a regular. One night, he was approached by a prostitute who knew him well from his previous way of life, but he walked right past her. In amazement, she called to him, 'Augustine, don't you recognize me? It's ME!' For a moment he stopped, then turned to her and said, 'Yes. But it's no longer me.'

The transformation that happens when we are converted is real and dramatic: the Bible describes it at various times as from darkness to light, from lost to found, from death to life. At our very core we are changed from fundamentally sinful to fundamentally righteous. Jesus' perfection becomes ours, and by it we can enter the most holy place of God's presence in worship. It is by his grace that we enter, not by our own holiness.

But another important aspect of worship is sanctification, of increasing holiness, whereby we are little by little being conformed to the image of Jesus in our daily lives. If we are truly to engage with God in worship, our hearts must be right with him and with one another; at this point, a lack of holiness through hardness of heart from unconfessed sin will create a barrier between us and God.

Do we have hardness of heart in any areas of our lives? Take some time for people to confess it to God, then perhaps spend a few more minutes thanking him for his forgiveness and grace.

# 16. The Wisdom of God

## INTRODUCTION

God knows everything. That's a pretty good qualification for making wise judgements! And God constantly makes wise decisions over our lives. The problem sometimes is that his ways are higher than ours, and therefore his wisdom significantly differs from ours! Let's worship the immortal, invisible, only wise God.

## ACTIVITY

'I wouldn't have done it like that.'

Many of us have stories we can tell of how God has clearly worked out circumstances or answered prayers in ways we did not expect, but which were for our own good.

Ask the group to share any such stories in their own lives, where the wisdom of God became clear with hindsight.

Then consider together God's intervention and involvement in redeeming humankind. How would you have done it? Would you have chosen a tiny, obscure nation (Israel), occupied by hostile forces and riven with political upheaval? Would you have sent your beloved Son, the Creator and Sustainer of all things, to be born to a teenager in a stable?

Would you have allowed him to die in agony?

Would you have started the church with fishermen and tax collectors? Would you have chosen *you* to continue the ministry of Jesus?

These questions should cause us some amazement. But we can also be thankful that his wisdom is so much greater than ours, not only in world history, but in our own lives.

## THANKSGIVING

- Your perfect wisdom is proved in your wonderful and complete plan of salvation.
- Our lives are an unfolding story of your love and faithfulness.
- We may not be able to understand or second-guess your ways, but we can trust you to work out all things perfectly.
- You have shared your wisdom with us, revealing your plans for the world, for the church, for Christ's return, and for our eternal future.

## DOXOLOGY (You could read this out together.)

Romans 11:33–34

*Oh, the depth of the riches of the wisdom and knowledge of God!*

*How unsearchable his judgments,*
*and his paths beyond tracing out!*
*'Who has known the mind of the Lord?*
*Or who has been his counsellor?'*

## KEY SCRIPTURES

### 1 Corinthians 1:24–25

*Christ [is] the power of God and the wisdom of God. For the foolishness of God is wiser than man's wisdom, and the weakness of God is stronger than man's strength.*

Your way is always wiser than the craftiest, most brilliant plan that we could devise. Teach us to seek your wisdom, not to rely on our own.

### 1 Corinthians 1:20

*Where is the wise man? Where is the scholar? Where is the philosopher of this age? Has not God made foolish the wisdom of the world?*

Human wisdom does not help us understand God. We don't need intelligence or knowledge to follow him; we need faith and a willing heart.

### Romans 8:26–27

*In the same way, the Spirit helps us in our weakness. We do not know what we ought to pray for, but the Spirit himself intercedes for us with groans that words cannot express. And he who searches our hearts knows the mind of the Spirit, because the Spirit intercedes for the saints in accordance with God's will.*

We are not on our own. We have the Holy Spirit, who speaks to us and guides us in our praying.

James 1:5

*If any of you lacks wisdom, he should ask God, who gives generously to all without finding fault, and it will be given to him.*

God will give us his wisdom if we ask.

SONGS (Disc 4)

1. Be Thou my vision
2. The crucible for silver
3. Now unto the King eternal
4. Come, Holy Spirit (*Instrumental*)

PRAYER

Lord, we acknowledge your absolute power and wisdom. We know that you always work for our good, and we look to you, not ourselves, to know what's best for us. As Solomon did, we ask for more wisdom, that we may live aright. Give us a greater understanding of you, and a greater fellowship with the Holy Spirit, that we may follow his leading in our thoughts, our actions and our decisions, and so better reflect your wisdom.

APPLICATION

Sometimes situations in our lives can cause us to doubt his wisdom: we feel he's forgotten us, that somehow he's not in control any more. This week, think about those circumstances, and spend time asking God to show you what you need to know of his plan in those areas; then trust him with it.

James 1:5 tells us to ask for wisdom. Get into the habit of asking him to guide you each time you have an important decision to make or counsel to give.

*Part 2: Jesus*

# 17. Jesus the Word

## INTRODUCTION

There are many pictures used in the Bible to describe Jesus. He employs several himself: the door, the good shepherd, living water, bread, the way, the truth, the life. But it is as the Word that the apostle John begins his gospel account, as he describes Jesus' eternal pre-existence.

This is an important passage for understanding the Son's relationship to the Father, and the authority he has held from the beginning. It also makes the act of coming to earth as a man all the more remarkable.

## ACTIVITY

Begin by reading the passage below from John 1:

*In the beginning was the Word, and the Word was with God, and the Word was God. He was with God in the beginning. Through him all things were made; without him nothing was made that has been made. In him was life, and that life was the light of men. The light shines in the darkness, but the darkness has not understood it . . . The Word became flesh and made his dwelling among us. We have seen his glory, the glory of the One and Only, who came from the Father, full of grace and truth.*

Discuss why it is appropriate to call Jesus the Word:

- He reveals the truth – words are there to tell us the truth.
- He shows us what God is like – through his words and actions on earth, Jesus was revealing God's character and purposes to us in the most complete way possible, because he is God.
- In the beginning, God spoke, and the creation came into being. Jesus was that 'word' through whom everything was made, and by whom it is sustained.

Begin to give thanks to Jesus for coming to earth to reveal the Father to us, and for providing the way back to him by his sacrifice.

## THANKSGIVING

- You are the giver and sustainer of life. Everything we see, hear and touch; everything we can think; every emotion – it has all come into being through you.
- You came to show us what the Father is like, and just how much he loves us.
- You became the voice of the Father for us, his perfect likeness on earth, displaying his character and revealing his glory.
- You speak today, and your words still have life-giving power.
- You continue to shine your light into our hearts.

## KEY SCRIPTURES

Hebrews 1:3

*The Son is the radiance of God's glory and the exact representation of his being, sustaining all things by his powerful word.*

You showed us the Father, gloriously and completely.

Psalm 19:1–6

*The heavens declare the glory of God;*
  *the skies proclaim the work of his hands.*
*Day after day they pour forth speech;*
  *night after night they display knowledge.*

Creation itself has been given a voice; it testifies to the One who made it, to your glory, your magnificence, your care, your constancy, and your power.

SONGS (Disc 4)

5. O sacred King
6. Lord, You have my heart
7. When the music fades (Heart of worship)
8. Jesu, joy of man's desiring (*Instrumental*)

PRAYER

Lord, we are so grateful that you were willing to lay aside your majesty and come to us, revealing the glory, the power and the love of God to sinful men and women. Thank you that you stopped at nothing to present us holy and blameless to the Father, even though it cost you everything. Amen.

REFLECTION

In his book *The Cross and the Switchblade* David Wilkerson tells of the time when Nicky Cruz threatened to cut him into a thousand pieces. David's response was: 'And every piece would say "I love you".' That's the powerful message of the

Word of God on the cross, which speaks across the centuries to every man, woman and child on earth. Jesus was God's message of love.

## APPLICATION

Words have power. Sometimes we remember things that were said to us even when we were small children, words which have helped to shape our lives. Sometimes these words have been negative, imprisoning us: 'you'll never be good at anything . . . you're so stupid . . . I hate you . . .'

Jesus came to free us from the lies and accusations of the evil one, whenever and however they have been spoken over us. As the Word of God, Jesus has already defeated the enemy. We can be set free, and healed of the hurt those words might have brought.

If there are those who feel they need prayer in this area, it is best to arrange to do this on another occasion, when specific counselling can take place.

# 18. Jesus, Alpha and Omega

## INTRODUCTION

One of the ways the Bible attempts to describe the complete-
ness of Jesus' rule and reign is using the phrase 'Alpha and
Omega'. Alpha and Omega are the first and last letters of the
Greek alphabet, so the parallel today would be to describe
Jesus as the 'A and the Z' – perhaps not quite as poetic,
though.

The simple activity below may help to bring the idea of
Jesus as the beginning and the end of all things into our
imagination.

## ACTIVITY

You will need a telephone directory.

Ask (for fun): 'What do you think is the first name in the
directory? And the last?'

Read the first and the last names from the directory. Ask:
'Are these people connected?' Probably not! The directory is
just a collection of names of people with no link except that
they have a phone. But each person represented has a personal history, a family background, a story of relationships,
hopes, disappointments, etc. And Jesus knows every story
inside out.

The Bible describes Jesus as the Alpha and Omega, in an attempt to describe his complete sovereignty and omniscience over the whole of history, from the very beginning to the very end of time itself. From the first ray of light to the last, from the first person to the last, and everyone in between, he rules over all.

Let's worship the One who is the Lord of every man and woman; the Lord of nations, races and cultures; the Lord of time; and the Lord of history.

## THANKSGIVING

- Human history is in your hands.
- You will reign for ever.
- You are above every rule and authority.
- You know me, and love me, completely.
- You know how everything will turn out.
- Our names are written in the Book of Life.

## KEY SCRIPTURES

Revelation 1:8

*'I am the Alpha and the Omega,' says the Lord God, 'who is, and who was, and who is to come, the Almighty.'*

Lord, your reign is complete. You can see the beginning from the end. Nothing comes as a surprise to you, and you cannot be caught out. Your rule is for ever, and we put our trust in you.

Revelation 21:6

*He said to me: 'It is done. I am the Alpha and the Omega, the Beginning and the End. To him who is thirsty I will give to drink without cost from the spring of the water of life.'*

We come to you, thirsty and poor, but knowing that your power is only matched by your love for us. You give freely and abundantly, and we are refreshed by your goodness to us.

Colossians 1:15–18

*He is the image of the invisible God, the firstborn over all creation. For by him all things were created: things in heaven and on earth, visible and invisible, whether thrones or powers or rulers or authorities; all things were created by him and for him. He is before all things, and in him all things hold together. And he is the head of the body, the church; he is the beginning and the firstborn from among the dead, so that in everything he might have the supremacy.*

Everything we can see, you made. Every military, political, or legal power; every demonic force, addiction, or emotional bondage; it's all subject to you, and you have total authority over it. You are indeed the King of kings and Lord of lords, and through your body, the church, you are advancing your kingdom on the earth.

Isaiah 43:1

*Fear not, for I have redeemed you;*
*I have summoned you by name; you are mine.*

If we belong to you, then we will not fear, for not even death can separate us from you.

## SONGS (Disc 4)

9. He is the Lord (Show Your power)
10. The King of love
11. Come, see this glorious Light (Blessing and honour)
12. Father in heaven, how we love You

## PRAYER

It's amazing to think that you, the Lord of history, should actually become part of it, entering our world as a man, and giving yourself as a sacrifice for those who had rejected you. We know that one day you will bring to an end what you began, bringing eternal salvation to those who trust in you, and eternal judgement to those who don't. You truly are the great Saviour and glorious Lord. Amen.

## APPLICATION

It's very easy to be preoccupied with the here and now, and forget that God has a greater plan and purpose that runs right through history, in which each one of us has an important part to play.

How should this eternal perspective affect the way we think and act in daily life?

# 19. Jesus, King of Kings

## INTRODUCTION

We regularly use the term 'King of kings' in relation to Jesus, even though in most societies today the position of king or queen doesn't hold the power it once did. Bearing in mind that the term indicates Jesus' position of power and authority over every earthly power and authority, it might be more appropriate to think of him as the 'President of presidents', or the 'Prime Minister of prime ministers'.

Of course, these posts don't hold the sense of supremacy and awe that an absolute monarch did in times gone by, but it might at least help to emphasize that Jesus' rule is as complete and relevant today as it ever was.

Here is an activity that uses the historic (and biblical) symbol of the crown as the mark of power and rule. It is intended to revitalize a title that can easily begin to lose its meaning for us and become jargon.

## ACTIVITY

You will need card and Sellotape (or a stapler), scissors and something to colour with, if your group is childlike enough to enjoy that sort of thing – definitely for a fun-loving group! Although you may find some resistance at first to this activity, it's worth persevering, as the symbolic act at the end can be quite powerful.

Begin by reading Psalm 2. You can read it out together if you all have the same translation, or alternatively read a couple of verses each. Consider the overwhelming supremacy of God over every ungodly power that would seek to challenge him.

Then read Psalm 8 together. See how God still gives dignity and authority to human beings, even those who would seek to flout his laws or deny his existence.

As a group, make crowns out of card. You can have them cut ready, or, if you want the group to enjoy more of the making process, you can all start with card and scissors (and coloured stickers, if you wish you were still invited to children's parties)! Alternatively, of course, you may have some Christmas crackers left over with ready-made crowns inside.

Encourage everybody to put on a 'crown' and consider together the wonder of being part of royalty, as those made in God's image (making every human royal) and now as a royal priesthood (1 Peter 2:9), bought with a price.

Then read Philippians 2:1–11. Consider the type of crown we know Jesus wore – made of thorns.

Take off your crowns as an act of worship and reverence and thank the Son of God for leaving his own royal status in order to restore ours.


THANKSGIVING

- You are head of every power and authority in heaven and hell, and on the earth. Nothing can overthrow your position, or thwart your purposes.
- You still give dignity and authority to men and women, even when they abuse it, and you hold back your wrath

and judgement, that all may have the opportunity to repent.

- You cause us to reign in the heavenlies with you, that we might exercise your power and authority and advance your kingdom on the earth.
- You were willing to lay aside your crown, and humble yourself to death on the cross.
- You were raised up again, to reign for ever as King of kings and Lord of lords!

## KEY SCRIPTURE

Philippians 2:9–11

*Therefore God exalted [Jesus] to the highest place*
*    and gave him the name that is above every name,*
*that at the name of Jesus every knee should bow,*
*    in heaven and on earth and under the earth,*
*and every tongue confess that Jesus Christ is Lord,*
*    to the glory of God the Father.*

One day everyone will acknowledge your position: for those who do it now, there is mercy, forgiveness and eternal life; for those who refuse, there is judgement and hell. Lord, use us to proclaim your greatness to the nations!

## SONGS (Disc 4)

13. Welcome, King of kings
14. All hail the Lamb
15. You laid aside Your majesty
16. Crown Him with many crowns (*Instrumental*)

## PRAYER

Lord, we are amazed by your grace: the King of kings, who willingly endured what we deserve in order that we might receive what you deserve – and all for the joy set before you, the joy of bringing us into your glorious kingdom. No wonder you were given the name that is above every other name! Amen!

## APPLICATION

**Either:**

Pray for those you know who don't acknowledge the rule of King Jesus. Ask God to soften their hearts, and to give you opportunities to share the gospel with them.

**Or:**

In today's competitive society, something that seems to be an increasingly important commodity is *status*. People are very preoccupied with where they stand in relation to one another – economically, socially, educationally, and in many other ways. But consider that amazing statement in Philippians 2:6 – '[Jesus], being in very nature God, did not consider equality with God something to be grasped.'

How much does status influence our attitudes: at work, in our family, at church, with our friends? Ask God to begin to identify and root out things in our lives that don't match up to the humble example of Christ.

# 20. Jesus, Name above All Names

## INTRODUCTION

The phrases 'in the name of Jesus' or 'in Jesus' name' appear a great deal in the Bible, and in our praying. But what does it mean to speak about Jesus' name?

In the Bible, as Wayne Grudem points out in his *Systematic Theology*, a person's name describes his character. So when we love Jesus' name, we are loving him, his character, and his ways. But we can go further. It also denotes his authority, the position he holds in the heavens as the Lord of all. So when we pray for healing or cast out demons in Jesus' name, we are calling upon his authority and power to accomplish the task.

Consequently, when we describe Jesus as the name above all names, not only is he the purest of the pure, the most loving of the loving, the strongest of the strong, and so on, he is also the authority over every other authority, the power that stands supreme over every other power. And, although he always has been God, it is as the result of his victory on the cross that *he has been given* the name above every other name.

## ACTIVITY

Test the general knowledge of your group with a short quiz. (In order to avoid being embarrassed, you may want to look up the answers first!)

1  Who is the president of the United States?
2  Who is the vice-president?
3  Who is the prime minister of Britain?
4  Who is Chancellor of the Exchequer?
5  Who is the president of Russia?
6  Who is the world's richest man?

Now ask the same questions, prefacing them with, 'Ten years ago, who was . . .' Ask: 'How many did we get? Of those we remembered, how many names have changed?' (Probably all of them.)

Point out that names come and go. While they are current, they can yield extraordinary power. But when they disappear, their power is lost, and they are, by and large, forgotten. Even the titles they hold change over time, as styles of government and countries' boundaries alter.

Jesus' name is different. No matter how powerful the politician, or sovereign, or military dictator, the name of Jesus is a higher authority and power. And whereas power, and the pursuit of power, is often a corrupting force in those people's lives, Jesus is utterly kind, loving and pure. We can trust him for his unchanging rule of justice and love.

## THANKSGIVING

- You rule over creation.
- You rule over every ruler and authority.

- You rule over every circumstance.
- Your power will never decrease; indeed, of the increase of your government there will be no end!
- Your character and authority are supreme over all.

## KEY SCRIPTURES

Ephesians 1:19–23

*[God's] power is like the working of his mighty strength, which he exerted in Christ when he raised him from the dead and seated him at his right hand in the heavenly realms, far above all rule and authority, power and dominion, and every title that can be given, not only in the present age but also in the one to come. And God placed all things under his feet and appointed him to be head over everything for the church, which is his body, the fulness of him who fills everything in every way.*

Jesus, you are placed far above all other rulers and authorities – in fact, they are under your feet! Your reign is for ever, and your power is supreme; yet you appoint the church to be the full expression of yourself here on earth, and work out your purposes through us. What a blessing, to have the fullness of Christ – all his riches and blessings – poured out upon us!

Philippians 2:9–11

*Therefore God exalted him to the highest place*
    *and gave him the name that is above every name,*
*that at the name of Jesus every knee should bow,*
    *in heaven and on earth and under the earth,*
*and every tongue confess that Jesus Christ is Lord,*
    *to the glory of God the Father.*

One day every tongue will confess you, and every knee will bow before you. Your kingship will be seen by those who love you, by those who hate you, and even by those who deny you exist.

Revelation 5:12

*In a loud voice they sang:*
*'Worthy is the Lamb, who was slain,*
*to receive power and wealth and wisdom and strength*
*and honour and glory and praise!'*

This is the constant cry of praise from heaven. Whatever precious possession, talent, status or strength any one of us may happen to have, our worship involves offering them up to him for his glory and service.

SONGS (Disc 4)

17. You have been given
18. He is exalted
19. He has been given
20. Jesus, Name above all names (*Instrumental*)

PRAYER

Thank you for your supreme power and unchanging love. Because of these two things we can trust you for every situation in our lives, and we need fear no earthly or spiritual authority that may seek to harm us. Thank you that you have given us your name and your authority to see your kingdom extended here on earth. We offer up all we have in recognition of your supreme authority in everything. Amen.

## APPLICATION

In what ways does God want us to help make a difference and extend his kingdom on earth this week, through (1) prayer, (2) words, (3) actions? Encourage each person to seek him for specific things.

# 21. Jesus the Living Water 1

## INTRODUCTION

In his teaching, Jesus used everyday objects and basic elements to describe himself. Not only would everyone be familiar with the images he was using; it also demonstrates how he wants to be at the very core of our everyday lives.

No doubt some of the images would have surprised, even shocked people. How could a man claiming to be the Son of the Most High God be anything so mundane as a door, or a shepherd? Yet Jesus had come not to exalt himself, but to preach a message of salvation and forgiveness to the lost.

## ACTIVITY

You will need a piece of paper, and something to write with.

Make a list together on the paper of all the uses we have for water in the course of a day, e.g. to make a cup of tea in the morning, to have a shower, to wash clothes, to cook with, to clean with, to run our central heating, etc. Note how essential water is to our daily existence. Briefly discuss what it would be like if your water supply was cut off, and how that would affect you through the day!

Consider what kind of benefits water gives us: refreshing, cleansing, warmth, essential sustaining of life. You could write them next to each usage on your list. Then discuss how the presence of Jesus, the life-giving water, in our lives mirrors these everyday uses. For example, he refreshes me when I am dry; he cleanses me from sin and guilt when I go astray; he sustains me through life, etc. Encourage people to give thanks for all Jesus is and does for us as the living water.

NOTE: People in your group may need to know the refreshing and cleansing power of Jesus in their lives right now. After people have given thanks and worshipped for a while, don't be afraid to pray for one another, or to call on God together for his touch; and don't be surprised if the Holy Spirit moves in an immediate, tangible way.

## THANKSGIVING

- Jesus, the sustainer and provider for our lives.
- Jesus, the One who refreshes and revives us.
- Jesus, the One who cleanses and restores us.

## KEY SCRIPTURES

John 7:37–38

*On the last and greatest day of the Feast, Jesus stood and said in a loud voice, 'If anyone is thirsty, let him come to me and drink. Whoever believes in me, as the Scripture has said, streams of living water will flow from within him.'*

Everyone is welcome. The only requirement is that we're thirsty. And when we drink, the indwelling Holy Spirit becomes a well of living water within us. This is not a passing blessing. This is a constant source of life and power for every day of our lives.

Ezekiel 47:9

*Swarms of living creatures will live wherever the river flows. There will be large numbers of fish, because this water flows there and makes the salt water fresh; so where the river flows everything will live.*

Lord, only your living water could miraculously make the salt water fresh! We want that water to flow in our lives, bringing life and power to all we do and all those we meet.

Psalm 23:3

*He restores my soul.*

When we feel discouraged by failure, crushed by disappointments, or even just worn out, we can come to the One who restores us inwardly. We can come again and again, knowing that there is fresh, life-giving water for us.

**See also**

Revelation 22:17 – the free gift of life-giving water is there, but we need to come to him for it.

Revelation 7:17 – one day he will lead us to springs of living water, and be our comforter.

SONGS (Disc 5)

1. Down the mountain (The river is here)
2. Blessed Jesus
3. River, wash over me (*Instrumental*)
4. Wash me clean

## PRAYER

Lord, you are so many things to us. Thank you for this wonderful picture you give us of yourself as the life-giver, the sustainer, the source of our refreshment, and the One who cleanses us of all our sin. You truly are water to our souls.

We all need more of your refreshing, cleansing and sustaining in our lives; so come by the power of your Holy Spirit and satisfy your thirsty children. Amen.

## APPLICATION

Consider Jeremiah 2:13:

*My people have committed two sins:*
*They have forsaken me,*
   *the spring of living water,*
*and have dug their own cisterns,*
   *broken cisterns that cannot hold water.*

God's people were not only guilty of failing to come to him, but also of seeking to find that water in things other than God.

How often do we fail to enjoy God's living water, not because it isn't available to us, but because we are looking to another source? It could be money, alcohol, material possessions, even a relationship. These things aren't wrong in themselves; but when we become dependent on them, or we exclude God from them, they become the cisterns we drink from, and ultimately they will leave us unsatisfied.

Take a few moments quietly to consider the 'cisterns' in our own lives, and then pray for God's help to put our dependence back on him alone as our living water.

# 22. Jesus the Living Water 2

## INTRODUCTION

Jesus often used everyday objects and basic elements of life to describe himself, and there is no more essential element for us than water. It covers two-thirds of the world's surface. It's the basic sign of life; without water, nothing can live.

Water occurs in many different forms on the earth, and the Bible is quick to pick up on a number of them, using them to demonstrate the many and varied ways that God interacts with his people. The activity below is intended to open our eyes to the wealth of life we have in him, and to encourage us to step out and receive more of his life-giving water.

## ACTIVITY

You will need a large piece of paper, and something to write with.

List together as many natural sources of water as you can think of. Your list might include

- streams
- rain
- waterfalls
- seas

- babbling brooks
- fountains
- wells
- geysers
- deep rivers
- still pools, etc.

Take some time to consider the characteristics of each one –
powerful, still, crashing, waves, etc. – and write them down.
Then discuss how they mirror the way the Father, Son and
Holy Spirit reveal themselves to us. For example, the sea
mirrors God's power or the coming of the Holy Spirit in
waves, or the still pools mirror his peace, etc.

Begin to give thanks for the ways in which God manifests
his love, faithfulness and power through the images of water,
and ask him to reveal himself in fresh ways in our lives.

NOTE: God can and does come to us in many different ways
– sometimes peacefully, sometimes forcefully, sometimes
with joy, sometimes with tears. We must not put God in a
box, and stipulate that he can come to us in certain ways but
not in others. Instead, we should expect him to come.

Build an expectation into your group that God wants to
come among us, not just at church, or later at home, but right
now. Whether individuals actually 'feel' anything is not the
main issue. People should not depend on feelings or sensa-
tions to believe that God is at work in them; but equally they
should not shun or fear them.

## THANKSGIVING

- Your refreshing water comes to us in so many different
  ways.

- You know the best way to refresh us.
- Your life-giving water is always freely available.

## KEY SCRIPTURES

Psalm 36:9

*For with you is the fountain of life;*
  *in your light we see light.*

There is no other place we can go for refreshment and life but to your renewing, cleansing, life-giving fountain.

Isaiah 58:11

*The Lord will guide you always;*
  *he will satisfy your needs in a sun-scorched land*
  *and will strengthen your frame.*
*You will be like a well-watered garden,*
  *like a spring whose waters never fail.*

You don't call us to retreat to a cool, shady region. You call us to be a well-watered garden in a sun-scorched land. Our refreshing is a testimony to the thirsty, that they can come and drink, too.

Isaiah 12:3

*With joy you will draw water*
  *from the wells of salvation.*

You not only give us water. By your Holy Spirit you place wells of salvation within us, and as we can constantly draw from them in daily life, your joy becomes our strength.

**See also**

John 4:14 – such is the power of God's change in our lives, he promises we will never thirst again.

## SONGS (Disc 5)

5. My first love
6. Jesus (Holy and anointed One)
7. Your love (Pour over me)
8. Here is love (*Instrumental*)

## PRAYER

Thank you, Lord, that the whole of creation speaks of your glory, and we can learn so much about you by examining the wonderful things you have made. Thank you, too, that these aspects of your character demonstrated in creation are also a living reality in our own experience. Keep opening our eyes to show us more of yourself, because we are so thirsty for you. We want to receive all you have for us. Amen.

## APPLICATION

John 4 talks about each of us having a spring of living water within us. How does having this constant source of water affect our daily lives? In what practical ways can we learn to drink from this water in every situation of life?

# 23. Jesus, Light of the World

## INTRODUCTION

The term 'Light of the world' is used three times in Scripture: twice to refer to Jesus, and once to refer to us. Although it's a familiar phrase, it's a dramatic picture of the world's need of Jesus, and the difference he makes to people's lives. And as he shines his light into our hearts, we too become instruments of life-changing power in the lives of those around us.

## ACTIVITY

You will need five or six candles and some matches.

Often, a visual representation of a familiar concept such as light can trigger a fresh revelation about God and what he has done. This activity is a different way of approaching what is otherwise a very familiar Bible passage.

Ask everyone to find John chapter 1 in their Bibles and give out the candles, keeping one for yourself. Then make the room fairly dark so that it is difficult to read. Light your candle and read verses 1–2. Light another person's candle from your own and ask them to read verses 3–4. That person then lights another person's candle, who reads verse 5. Do the same with all the candles, reading a verse or two at a time, until all the candles are lit. By then it should be light enough for everyone to read up to the end of verse 13 together.

Briefly discuss the effect of lighting the candles – the significant difference each candle made, the way it literally illuminated the truth, etc. Then pray together, thanking God for sending the Light so that we could become children of God.

## THANKSGIVING

- You shone your light into the darkness of our lives.
- We are now children of light, shining in a dark world.
- You freed us from the slavery of guilt and sin, so we can walk in the light.
- Your light shows us the right way to live.

## KEY SCRIPTURES

Matthew 4:16

*The people living in darkness*
  *have seen a great light;*
*on those living in the land of the shadow of death*
  *a light has dawned.*

Your light has given hope to us, when all we knew was the darkness of a life bound by sin, lived in the shadow of a fearful death.

John 8:12

*When Jesus spoke again to the people, he said, 'I am the light of the world. Whoever follows me will never walk in darkness, but will have the light of life.'*

Your promise is that darkness will never again dominate our lives, for your light now shines in our hearts by the Holy Spirit.

## Matthew 5:14

*You are the light of the world. A city on a hill cannot be hidden.*

This light that shines in us, also shines out into a world of darkness. We cannot help but be lights in a dark place!

## Philippians 2:14–15

*Do everything without complaining or arguing, so that you may become blameless and pure, children of God without fault in a crooked and depraved generation, in which you shine like stars in the universe.*

Fostering an attitude of thanksgiving and fellowship, not complaining and arguing, is a powerful, bright testimony.

**See also**

1 John 1:7 – walking in the light not only brings purity into our lives, but it brings us closer to one another.

Ephesians 5:8 – we are children of light.

Matthew 5:16 – our light shines brightly by imitating Christ in humility, power and acts of kindness.

SONGS (Disc 5)

  9. We want to see Jesus lifted high
10. And He shall reign
11. O Jesus, Son of God (Light of the world)
12. Great is the darkness (Come, Lord Jesus)

PRAYER

Thank you for shining your light into our hearts, giving us hope, salvation, a clear conscience, and power to live aright for you. Let your light shine through us into others' hearts, that they may find you as their light and salvation. Amen.

APPLICATION

Two of the Bible references we have looked at mention not just being light, but walking in the light. We shine brightest when the way we live matches up to who we are. Just as there is no darkness at all in God, so our lives should be the same. Now, we are all aware of the 'big sins', like murder, stealing, and so on. But consider together what less obvious forms of darkness there could be in our lives:

- A lack of complete honesty
- Little acts of selfishness
- Ignoring someone else's need
- A lack of thankfulness to God
- Taking others for granted
- Hurtful comments to others
- Not expressing love to 'loved ones'

Take a moment individually to confess to God the little darknesses, and ask God to help you live truly in the light.

## 24. Jesus the Bread of Life

### INTRODUCTION

Jesus often used everyday objects and elements of life to describe how he wants to fill and satisfy us. Bread has a universal significance across many different cultures, and it is a central feature of our celebration of the Lord's Supper. So it is particularly appropriate that we examine the significance of the image Jesus used to help us understand him.

### ACTIVITY

You will need a loaf of bread, a glass of wine/blackcurrant juice, a notebook, and something to write with.

Put the loaf in the middle of the group. Remind everybody that Jesus said: 'I am the bread of life.'

Ask: 'Why did Jesus choose to describe himself as bread; not honey or meat or something else?'

Explore the qualities of bread together: basic, staple diet, suitable with every meal, easily obtained, the food that is handed out to refugees, filling, satisfying etc. Write down the words and phrases people use as they discuss this.

Read your notes back to the group, asking them to bear in mind just how much Jesus Christ is like bread. Then encourage people to talk to Jesus and thank him for what he means to them as the bread of life.

At an appropriate point in your time of worship, break bread and take wine together, reading out the 1 Corinthians scripture below. Try not to be too formal or 'religious'!

## THANKSGIVING

- You satisfy our hunger, and give us strength to walk in your ways.
- You invite us to taste and see that you are good.
- Bread reminds us of your sacrificial love, which drove you to the cross, where your body was broken and your blood was poured out for us.

## KEY SCRIPTURES

John 6:35

*Then Jesus declared, 'I am the bread of life. He who comes to me will never go hungry, and he who believes in me will never be thirsty.'*

Lord, your invitation is to come and be satisfied. We come to you, believing only you can satisfy us, for we know you are good, and we know you only give good things to your children.

Isaiah 55:1

*Come, all you who are thirsty,*
*    come to the waters;*
*and you who have no money,*
*    come, buy and eat!*
*Come, buy wine and milk*
*    without money and without cost.*

Such is the measure of your grace to us, the only requirement we need is to be hungry and broke!

### 1 Corinthians 11:23–25

*For I received from the Lord what I also passed on to you: The Lord Jesus, on the night he was betrayed, took bread, and when he had given thanks, he broke it and said, 'This is my body, which is for you; do this in remembrance of me.' In the same way, after supper he took the cup, saying, 'This cup is the new covenant in my blood; do this, whenever you drink it, in remembrance of me.'*

The symbol of your great sacrifice; the Lord of glory – the One the angels call holy, the One at whose name the demons flee – breaks his body, sheds his blood . . . and he does it for me.

### SONGS (Disc 5)

13. O taste and see
14. Giver of grace
15. See Him come (His body was broken)
16. We break this bread

### PRAYER

Thank you for all you mean to us as the bread of life. Thank you that you sustain and satisfy us, and just like the manna from heaven, each day there's also more! Amen.

### APPLICATION

From the description of life in the early church in Acts 2, 'breaking bread' seems to have been a more regular, informal

# Songs of Fellowship

## FOR SMALL GROUPS

*The complete resource for small group worship*

- 50 Worship Ideas for Small Groups – **The Book**

  A new book from Stuart Townend, bursting with 50 fresh ideas to get your small groups worshipping.

  **£8.99**

- Songs of Fellowship for Small Groups – **The Songsheet**

  200 songs and hymns, carefully selected for their suitability in small group worship, set out in an easy-to-read, A4 format.

  **£12.00 pack of 10**

- Songs of Fellowship for Small Groups – **The CDs**

  5 CDs featuring the first 100 songs included in the songsheet and book. Each track is especially suitable for use in the small group.

  **£24.99 introductory price**
  (£29.99 from Jan 1st 2001)

  Five more CDs following in Autumn 2000 include the 100 other songs from the songsheet

- **AND THE BEST NEWS OF ALL...**

  All these elements are included in a single pack! Everything you need for small group worship in one place.

  **£39.99 introductory price**
  (£49.99 from Jan 1st 2001)

For more details on this exciting new resource contact your local Christian Bookshop or in case of difficulty telephone 01273 234567. Or contact us at: Kingsway, 26 Lottbridge Drove, Eastbourne, BN23 6NT, England. Tel: (01323) 437700. Email: sales@kingsway.co.uk.

activity in the life of the early church than it is now, often happening in homes as part of a shared meal. Jesus also tells us to remember him *whenever* we eat bread or drink wine. The implication seems to be that we should bring the celebration of Christ into our everyday activity of eating and drinking, as opposed to bringing eating and drinking into our celebration of Christ.

This week, use the start of mealtimes – whether as a family, with friends, or on your own – as an act of communion. Use food and drink that everyone can share in (not necessarily bread and wine), and spend a few moments giving thanks to God, celebrating the death and resurrection of Christ, and expressing our unity in him.

## 25. Jesus the Vine

### INTRODUCTION

The picture of the vine and the vineyard is not one that is particularly common in the cooler climates of the West, but it would have been a common sight in biblical times. Jesus was fond of using real, down-to-earth images and metaphors to explain God's character and purposes. Not only would people easily understand and relate to it; he wanted to demonstrate that God is not a distant, spiritual figure inviting us into an ascetic, other-worldly life. He is the God of the practical, the everyday, bringing life, power and meaning to the nitty-gritty of our lives.

### ACTIVITY

You will need any kind of plant, preferably one with a single stem and branches coming off it.

Place the plant in full view of everyone. Explain that vines are rather difficult to get hold of in our climate, but plants work by the same principle!

Ask: 'How did this plant begin its life? How did it grow? How do the leaves and flowers get their nourishment? Why are all the leaves/flowers of the same kind?'

Read out John 15:1–8. Allow people to consider the

passage, and encourage them to share any thoughts or questions they have about it.

Jesus pictures himself as the core of the plant. We are the branches, and the flowers and leaves are the 'fruit' of our lives. As branches we have the plant's 'genetic imprint', causing us to produce fruit in keeping with the plant itself. If we keep drawing from the life-giving Source, 'abiding in the vine', we will bear fruit.

Note that it is a natural process. Fruit is the result of healthy growing. A lack of fruit is not a sign of not trying hard enough. It's a result of not being in touch with the vine.

Let's spend a few moments abiding with Jesus in worship, enjoying his presence, expressing our love to him, and allowing the Holy Spirit to lead us.

## THANKSGIVING

- We are sons and daughters of the living God, brought from death to life, reborn with your 'genetic imprint'.
- Jesus, you are a constant source of life-giving nourishment for us, giving us all we need for life and godliness.
- You are faithful and constant in leading us, guiding us, and causing us to grow.
- Abiding in you is such joy!

## KEY SCRIPTURES

Psalm 1:1–3

*Blessed is the man*
   *who does not walk in the counsel of the wicked*
*or stand in the way of sinners*
   *or sit in the seat of mockers.*

*But his delight is in the law of the Lord,*
  *and on his law he meditates day and night.*
*He is like a tree planted by streams of water,*
  *which yields its fruit in season*
*and whose leaf does not wither.*
  *Whatever he does prospers.*

Your promise is that as we walk uprightly, and feed on your word, we become firmly planted and nourished in you, and we are fruitful in everything. Thank you for your life-giving power.

Jeremiah 17:8

*He will be like a tree planted by the water*
  *that sends out its roots by the stream.*
*It does not fear when heat comes;*
  *its leaves are always green.*
*It has no worries in a year of drought*
  *and never fails to bear fruit.*

It's our roots that cause the fruit to grow in the time of drought. We need to learn to put down solid roots in the times of blessing, so that they may sustain us when trouble and hardship come.

Galatians 5:22–23

*But the fruit of the Spirit is love, joy, peace, patience, kindness, goodness, faithfulness, gentleness and self-control. Against such things there is no law.*

Lord, we want these things to characterize our lives. But you don't want us to be motivated by guilt or a sense of duty. You

want us to have fellowship with you by the Holy Spirit.
Teach us to abide in you daily.

## SONGS (Disc 5)

17. I will rest in Christ
18. Jesus, lover of my soul (It's all about You)
19. By Your side
20. Jesus take me as I am (*Instrumental*)

## QUOTE FOR PARENTS

Children are a gift from God for the shaping of your character!

## PRAYER

Lord, we love to abide in you. Thank you that you are committed to causing the fruit of your Spirit to grow in our lives.
Teach us the secret of drawing on you in our daily walk, of
allowing your life to flow from us in all we do. Amen.

## APPLICATION

John 15 talks about the Father cutting off branches that
don't bear fruit, and pruning those that do, so they can
bear more fruit. In what areas do you feel God is 'pruning'
your life, making you more fruitful and therefore more like
Jesus?

It can be very helpful to identify these areas, as often it
helps to make sense of certain circumstances and events in
our lives that otherwise leave us confused and discouraged.
We can begin to see that God is indeed working for our own
good, even if it is painful at the time.

Encourage people to write down these relevant areas in their lives, so that they can pray through them later, on their own, and refer to them in the coming months. It may also be helpful to individuals if you (or another member of the group) were to follow through these situations with them as they progress. As members of one body, we are called to bear one another's burdens.

# 26. Unto Us a Child Is Born

## INTRODUCTION

Once a year we turn our thoughts to the birth of Jesus; but all too often the wonder of this awesome event is obscured by the trappings of Christmas – holidays, presents, food, television, etc.

It is worth having a much closer look at the wonder of God coming to earth as a baby.

## ACTIVITY

If you have any photos of babies or toddlers (or even a real one in person!), let the group have a quick look at them. Consider the 'life' of a baby – what are the characteristics of babyhood (total dependence for warmth, food and affection; languageless; everything is 'new'; inability to move where you want to; nappies, teething, etc.)? Ask the group to offer ideas, as you make notes.

Read the list back to the group and marvel together that the eternal Son of God submitted himself to the state of babyhood. Read the quote below, then choose one or two of the scriptures to read, to lead you into prayer and worship.

## QUOTE

The God who roared, who could order armies and empires about like pawns on a chessboard, this God emerged in Palestine as a baby who could not speak or eat solid food or control his bladder, who depended on a teenage couple for shelter, food, and love.

Philip Yancey
*The Jesus I Never Knew* (Fount, 1999)

## THANKSGIVING

- You were willing to lay aside everything – your glory, your position, your power – for our sake.
- You were obedient to your Father in coming to earth.
- In coming to earth as a helpless baby, not only were you trusting yourself to a young, inexperienced couple, but you were making yourself vulnerable to the attack of the devil (through Herod). And yet you trusted your Father to keep you safe.

## KEY SCRIPTURES

Isaiah 9:6 (NASB)

*For a child will be born to us, a son will be given to us;*
*And the government will rest on His shoulders;*
*And His name will be called Wonderful Counselor, Mighty God,*
*Eternal Father, Prince of Peace.*

Given this wonderful description, readers of the Old Testament could be forgiven for expecting a glorious, triumphal entry into the world for the Messiah. Jesus chose the way of obscurity, of humility and servanthood; yet those who seek him will find him to be the glorious Messiah described here.

## John 1:14

*The Word became flesh and made his dwelling among us. We have seen his glory, the glory of the One and Only, who came from the Father, full of grace and truth.*

When you came to earth, all you brought was yourself. Without the accoutrements of splendour or power, all we saw was the essential character of God – full of grace and truth. And even in that, the glory of God shone through.

## Philippians 2:6–8

*Who, being in very nature God,*
  *did not consider equality with God something to be grasped,*
*but made himself nothing,*
  *taking the very nature of a servant,*
  *being made in human likeness.*
*And being found in appearance as a man,*
  *he humbled himself*
  *and became obedient to death – even death on a cross!*

So often we have little to boast about, yet we choose to be arrogant. You had everything to boast about, yet you chose to be humble.

## Hebrews 2:9

*But we see Jesus, who was made a little lower than the angels, now crowned with glory and honour because he suffered death, so that by the grace of God he might taste death for everyone.*

Jesus' glory is even greater because of his willingness to humble himself.

## SONGS (Disc 6)

1. Joy to the world
2. Meekness and majesty
3. From heaven You came (The Servant King)
4. O come and join the dance (*Instrumental*)

Alternatively, you could sing some well-known carols together, if it's Christmas – or even if it isn't!

## PRAYER

Lord, we are humbled by your humility. You not only chose to come to us, but to become one of us, born a weak and vulnerable baby, and growing up knowing the joys, sorrows and dangers that make up all of our lives. Thank you for making yourself the gift of salvation for a sinful world. Amen.

## APPLICATION

We are probably aware of how sanitized our view is of Jesus' birth these days – Christmas cards depicting soft scenes in a warm, even homely stable, and so on. But do we appreciate the scandal of the situation? Imagine the rumours and gossip in a tight-knit community when an unmarried girl becomes pregnant, refusing to name the father, even claiming that it's a miracle of God!

How much are we influenced by what others think of us? How quick are we to judge others? Pray with one another for strength to stand up for the right thing, even when it's unpopular, and for grace to love rather than judge.

# 27. Immanuel

## INTRODUCTION

One of the most astounding features of the Christian faith, and one that sets it apart from all the other main religions, is summed up in the word 'Immanuel', which simply means 'God with us'.

That God should love and care for us is wonderful. That he should desire us to know him through a personal, loving relationship is staggering. But to demonstrate this by coming to earth himself and becoming a human being – that is almost too mind-blowing to take in.

And yet when Isaiah prophesied that the virgin would be with child, and that the child would be called Immanuel – that is literally what God did.

## ACTIVITY

You will need some sweet-smelling flowers, or a bottle of perfume; a spare room.

Put some perfume or some flowers in a room which is not your meeting room. Ask a member of the group to go into the other room and describe the smell of the perfume or the smell and appearance of the flowers in as much detail as possible.

Ask members of the group what they think the smell (and

appearance of the flowers) is like. Allow them to struggle with the difficulty of the question!

Now ask the person in the other room to put some perfume on and come into the room (or bring the flowers in). Invite everyone to smell the perfumed wrist or flowers and encourage them to express their reactions. Ask everyone to consider the difference in quality of the two experiences and why the second was better.

Explain that this is precisely what the Father did through Jesus. Read Hebrews 1:1–4, and encourage everyone to worship the God who actually came and dwelt among us in Jesus, and still comes to us today by the Spirit.

## THANKSGIVING

- You didn't just choose words or feelings to reveal yourself to us – you came in flesh and blood.
- You gave us the most concrete example possible of how to live a holy life.
- You bought us with the price of your Son, that we might know you and be with you for ever.
- Jesus, you were willing to endure rejection, suffering and ultimately the cross for our sake.
- Your fragrance is now with us by the Holy Spirit, and we in turn as your body on earth become the fragrance of Christ to a sinful world.

## KEY SCRIPTURES

### John 1:14

*The Word became flesh and made his dwelling among us. We have seen his glory, the glory of the One and Only, who came from the Father, full of grace and truth.*

The One through whom all things were created, and by whom all things are sustained, came and lived among us; he revealed his glory as he ate, slept, laughed and cried as one of us.

1 John 4:12–13

*No-one has ever seen God; but if we love one another, God lives in us and his love is made complete in us. We know that we live in him and he in us, because he has given us of his Spirit.*

We now have God the Holy Spirit dwelling within us. Not a Spirit who rests upon us for a moment, then leaves. But one who walks with us, comforting, counselling, giving us strength, teaching, guiding, and powerfully working within us to make us more like Jesus. Thank the Lord for his wonderful Holy Spirit.

Revelation 21:3–4

*And I heard a loud voice from the throne saying, 'Now the dwelling of God is with men, and he will live with them. They will be his people, and God himself will be with them and be their God. He will wipe every tear from their eyes. There will be no more death or mourning or crying or pain, for the old order of things has passed away.'*

Right now he is with us. One day we will be with him – face to face, in the presence of his glory, and free from the restraints of a fallen world. That is where we were made to be.

SONGS (Disc 6)

5. The cross has said it all
6. May the fragrance of Jesus
7. From the squalor
8. Breathe on me, breath of God (*Instrumental*)

## PRAYER

Lord, it's amazing to think that you should come to earth at all. What's more incredible is that you should choose to do it by becoming one of us – a baby, a child, a teenager, a man, becoming the ultimate expression of the character of God through all the joys and sorrows, limitations and temptations of human existence. Then finally you endured the worst that sinful men could do to you – and all for our sake.

Thank you that, just as you walked with your disciples 2,000 years ago, you walk with us now by your Spirit, and we can know that same wonder, friendship and love of Immanuel, God with us. And one day you will call us home, and we will be face to face with you for ever. Amen.

## APPLICATION

Some people will be familiar with the campaign of booklets, wristbands, and so on, reminding us to check our thoughts, actions and decisions against the question 'What would Jesus do?' Remembering that we are not just imitating Christ, but that he is actually walking alongside us every day, how will that affect how we live this week? Encourage people to be specific about where words, thoughts and actions need to change.

# 28. Jesus the Man

## INTRODUCTION

It's one of the most amazing aspects of the gospel that Jesus, while being fully God, chose at the same time to become fully man: to become one of us, live among us, and die for us. We can often dwell so much on his divinity that we fail to appreciate how much he was just 'one of us', with the same joys, frustrations, temptations and emotions as us. In every sense, he really did 'walk our road'.

## ACTIVITY

Look up the following scriptures, and discuss how each one reveals Jesus' humanity:

Matthew 26:37 (sorrow and distress)
Matthew 26:38 (needing his friends)
Hebrews 12:2–3 (joy)
1 Peter 2:4 (rejection)
Matthew 14:14 (compassion)
John 11:35 (grief)
John 2:15 (anger)

Begin to thank Jesus that he was willing to lay aside his majesty, to humble himself and share in our humanity and lowliness, in order that we might be raised up with him to share in his glory.

## THANKSGIVING

- You were willing to lay aside all your glory, power and majesty for us.
- You came into the world in total obscurity and vulnerability.
- You were tempted in all the ways we are, but you came through without sin.
- You suffered the lowest degradation that man could put you through – shame, suffering and death.
- You rose from the dead as a man, and are now seated at the right hand of God as the man Christ Jesus.
- You intercede continually for us.

## KEY SCRIPTURES

Philippians 2:6–8

*Who, being in very nature God,*
*    did not consider equality with God something to be grasped,*
*but made himself nothing,*
*    taking the very nature of a servant,*
*    being made in human likeness.*
*And being found in appearance as a man,*
*    he humbled himself*
*    and became obedient to death – even death on a cross!*

You were willing to let go, to give up everything you had to serve those you had made. What an example of selfless humility!

## Hebrews 4:15 (NASB)

*For we do not have a high priest who cannot sympathize with our weaknesses, but One who has been tempted in all things as we are, yet without sin.*

Every kind of temptation we can think of, Jesus would have experienced it. Greed, lust, jealousy, arrogance, self-justification, lying – they all would have come to Jesus' door. But he would not give in to them.

## 1 Corinthians 10:13

*No temptation has seized you except what is common to man. And God is faithful; he will not let you be tempted beyond what you can bear. But when you are tempted, he will also provide a way out so that you can stand up under it.*

Father, you know how far we can go. You do not enjoy seeing us struggle, any more than you took pleasure in Jesus' wilderness temptations. But you know that victory over temptation is part of our character-shaping, part of our maturing into a greater likeness to Christ.

## SONGS (Disc 6)

9. I will offer up my life
10. Who can ever say they understand?
11. What kind of love is this?
12. The world is looking for a hero (Champion)

## PRAYER

Thank you, Lord, that you were willing to humble yourself for our sake, to take on human form and experience all the emotions and temptations that we face. We are amazed that you loved us so much that you would embrace our human experience, suffer and die, that we might have life. Thank you that, because you humbled yourself, we were raised with you and are seated with you in heavenly places. Thank you for the Holy Spirit, who gives us grace in our weakness, and helps us to live each day in your victory. Amen.

## APPLICATION

When we consider Jesus' victory over temptation, we are inclined to assume that somehow Jesus was at an advantage over us. Perhaps it was easier for him. After all, he was the Son of God. And of course, he didn't have the complex pressures of modern society to cope with.

But to think that way is to misunderstand both the completeness of Jesus' humanity, and the power of our own salvation. Jesus wasn't a divine example that we are to admire from afar. He was a man who lived according to the leading of the Spirit, the same Spirit that lives in every believer. His temptations were real, yet he came through. That same power that sustained him, and ultimately raised him from the dead, is at work in us.

God is committed to making us like Jesus. Before we became Christians, we couldn't help but sin; we were slaves, spiritually dead, and unable even to see the light, let alone walk in it. Now we have been born again, and made alive in Christ; the old self has been put to death, and the new has come. We have a completely new spirit within us that is a slave to righteousness, not a slave to sin.

True, we need to battle to overcome our flesh (just as Jesus did), for our flesh has not yet been regenerated (that comes later!). And we need to renew our minds constantly from our old way of thinking. But we have all we need for life and godliness. This is the glorious message of the gospel!

Consider some of the pressures and temptations that you have faced this week. If appropriate, ask people to share them, and pray for one another, asking for the same grace that was on Jesus to 'win through' in those situations.

# 29. The Example of Christ

## INTRODUCTION

We are probably all aware that Jesus' life is an example for us to follow. And we try to follow that example by being more patient, more loving, and sharing the gospel where we can.

But the closer we look at Jesus' life, the more amazing it appears to be. Words like 'shocking', 'radical', and 'exciting' appear alongside the more familiar 'caring', 'loving' descriptions; and they can cause us to worship and adore him in greater measure, as well as challenging us to follow his example.

## QUOTE

> [Jesus] was not at all like the psychologist's picture of the integrated, balanced, adjusted, happily married, employed, popular citizen. You can't really be very well 'adjusted' to your world if it says you 'have a devil' and ends by nailing you up naked to a stake of wood.
>
> C. S. Lewis
> *The Four Loves* (Geoffrey Bles, 1960)

## ACTIVITY

You will need a large sheet of paper, preferably stuck to a wall, and something to write with.

Have the following passages read out (or choose your own from the numerous examples in the gospels), and discuss what it shows us about the character of Jesus. Write the key descriptive words on the sheet of paper. Then, when you have finished, encourage people to use this as a basis for worship and adoration by prayer and singing:

Mark 6:34 (had compassion, was sensitive to people's needs)
Luke 18:15–17 (gave his attention to all ages)
Luke 19:1–9 (accepted and spent time with those the world rejected)
Matthew 21:12–13; 23:33 (showed righteous anger at hypocrisy)
John 8:1–11; Luke 23:34 (showed forgiveness and mercy to sinners)
Luke 6:12 (man of prayer)
Mark 2:15–16 (not concerned with reputation, spent time with the needy)
Luke 9:51 (determined to accomplish the task)
John 13:1–5 (servanthood and love)

## THANKSGIVING

- You came to earth to share completely in our humanity.
- You gave us your example of how to live – with love, joy, courage, compassion, tenderness, humour, sensitivity and humility.
- You gave us the Holy Spirit, who is at work in us, changing us more and more into your likeness.
- You give us the power to do the works that you did on earth.

## KEY SCRIPTURES

### Matthew 11:28–30

*Come to me, all you who are weary and burdened, and I will give you rest. Take my yoke upon you and learn from me, for I am gentle and humble in heart, and you will find rest for your souls. For my yoke is easy and my burden is light.*

Lord, thank you that your burden is not heavy. Being like you is not a hard graft, but a joyful submission to the work of your Spirit within us. We are weak, but our weakness enables you to be strong in us.

### 2 Corinthians 8:9

*For you know the grace of our Lord Jesus Christ, that though he was rich, yet for your sakes he became poor, so that you through his poverty might become rich.*

What an example! How willing are we to become poor, so that through it someone else might become rich? Ask God to teach us what it means to live this way, whatever the cost.

### Philippians 2:5–8

*Your attitude should be the same as that of Christ Jesus:*
*Who, being in very nature God,*
  *did not consider equality with God something to be*
  *grasped,*
*but made himself nothing,*
  *taking the very nature of a servant,*
  *being made in human likeness.*
*And being found in appearance as a man,*
  *he humbled himself*
  *and became obedient to death – even death on a cross!*

You deserved glory; yet you chose service. You deserved respect; yet you chose humility; you deserved justice; yet you chose forgiveness. Lord, make a change in my heart to choose the way of the cross.

## 2 Corinthians 3:18

*And we, who with unveiled faces all reflect the Lord's glory, are being transformed into his likeness with ever-increasing glory, which comes from the Lord, who is the Spirit.*

This transformation comes not from ourselves, but from you. It is your work from beginning to end, and it only requires our co-operation and obedience.

## SONGS (Disc 6)

13. You came from heaven to earth
14. He came to earth (King of kings)
15. Jesus Christ (Once again)
16. Jesus, all for Jesus

## PRAYER

Lord, thank you for the amazing example you set as you lived on earth. We need your grace and your Spirit to continue the work of being Christ to one another and to a needy world. Please help us to love as you loved, forgive as you forgave, and serve as you served. Amen.

## APPLICATION

Think about the passage in John 13 when Jesus washed the disciples' feet. In those days, washing feet was the job of the lowest person in the household and Jesus' act was a demonstration of servanthood which those present could immediately relate to.

Today, in Western culture, it is hard to think of a similar activity that could demonstrate the point that Jesus wanted to make. However, if you have a few colours of shoe polish, you could offer to clean (or more likely insist on cleaning) any of the group members' shoes after reading the passage together.

Alternatively, propose that a few of you wash a group member's car while that person has a cup of tea or coffee. Read John 13 again together and then discuss other ways of following Jesus' example of servanthood to your families, each other, and friends and neighbours.

NOTE: You may feel that these activities – the first one in particular – would be embarrassing to members of your group. But before you dismiss them out of hand . . . how embarrassed do you think the disciples felt when their teacher and master became the equivalent of their 'shoe-shine boy'? For that very reason it may bring home to people the full significance of Jesus' actions, and stir us to be genuinely more serving to one another.

# 30. The Cross

## INTRODUCTION

We're going to meditate on the final hours of Jesus' life. It's important to do this, not to be morbid or to upset ourselves, but in order to appreciate the immense cost of the cross. The more we appreciate his sacrifice, the more we will want to worship him with all our hearts.

## ACTIVITY

The following meditation can be done in a single room, but it's more effective when you are able to spread out into different rooms in the house. 'Allocate' parts of the room or rooms where you meet (and perhaps the garden) as Gethsemane, the praetorium, and Golgotha.

Tell the group in advance what each place represents, and, as you walk there, you or someone else read the appropriate passage – and, if practical, sing one or more of the songs. Then walk to the next place to read the next passage. You may want to hold a lit candle, which you blow out when someone reads that Jesus gave up his spirit.

As the scriptures are read out, encourage people to imagine the scene, and how Jesus felt. You may also feel it is appropriate to share bread and wine together informally, as you remember his death, celebrate the unity of the body, and look for his return.

(Walk to the first place.)


## IN GETHSEMANE

Matthew 26:38–39

*Then he said to them, 'My soul is overwhelmed with sorrow to the point of death. Stay here and keep watch with me.'*

*Going a little farther, he fell with his face to the ground and prayed, 'My Father, if it is possible, may this cup be taken from me. Yet not as I will, but as you will.'*


SONG (Disc 6)
17.  He was pierced (Like a lamb)

(Walk to the second place.)


## MOCKED AND HUMILIATED

Matthew 27:27–31

*Then the governor's soldiers took Jesus into the Praetorium and gathered the whole company of soldiers around him. They stripped him and put a scarlet robe on him, and then twisted together a crown of thorns and set it on his head. They put a staff in his right hand and knelt in front of him and mocked him. 'Hail, king of the Jews!' they said. They spit on him, and took the staff and struck him on the head again and again. After they had mocked him, they took off the robe and put his own clothes on him. Then they led him away to crucify him.*


SONG (Disc 6)
18.  Come and see (We worship at Your feet)

(Walk to the third place.)


## ON THE CROSS

### Matthew 27:33–37

*They came to a place called Golgotha (which means The Place of the Skull). There they offered Jesus wine to drink, mixed with gall; but after tasting it, he refused to drink it. When they had crucified him, they divided up his clothes by casting lots. And sitting down, they kept watch over him there. Above his head they placed the written charge against him:* THIS IS JESUS, THE KING OF THE JEWS.


### SONG (Disc 6)
19. O sacred head once wounded (*Instrumental*)


## JESUS' DEATH

### Matthew 27:45–50

*From the sixth hour until the ninth hour darkness came over all the land. About the ninth hour Jesus cried out in a loud voice, 'Eloi, Eloi, lama sabachthani?' – which means, 'My God, my God, why have you forsaken me?'*

*When some of those standing there heard this, they said, 'He's calling Elijah.'*

*Immediately one of them ran and got a sponge. He filled it with wine vinegar, put it on a stick, and offered it to Jesus to drink. The rest said, 'Now leave him alone. Let's see if Elijah comes to save him.'*

*And when Jesus had cried out again in a loud voice, he gave up his spirit.*

(If you have a candle, blow it out.)

SONG (Disc 6)
20. How deep the Father's love

PRAYER

Lord, we are awed and humbled by the suffering you went through. You, the Lord of heaven and earth, endured the shame and agony of the cross for the joy that was set before you – the joy of redeeming us, and having us with you for ever.

We are so thankful to you for your amazing sacrifice. But we are also filled with joy, for you have risen, defeating death, and declaring your eternal victory over sin and the devil. Now we look for your return, knowing that we will be with you for ever. Amen.

APPLICATION

Are we truly aware of the price that was paid for our sin? It's easy just to take for granted that our sins will be forgiven, and therefore adopt a rather casual attitude towards our wrong actions. Although we should never feel condemned about our sin, at the same time we should view it seriously, and ask for God's help to make our actions line up with what he wants.

Take a moment to consider the areas of our lives that God wants us to change, and ask for his grace to help us.

# 31. The Resurrection

## INTRODUCTION

The resurrection is the final act of victory in the story of salvation. As believers, we tend to marvel at the fact that God himself could come to earth to live among us, and allow himself to die on a cross. Most unbelievers marvel that a man could come back from the dead!

In no way should the resurrection diminish our appreciation of what the cross cost the Lord. Although Jesus was trusting the Father to raise him to life, the enormity of the horror – taking the punishment for every sin ever committed – can only be hinted at by Jesus' anguish in Gethsemane. It only makes his resurrection all the more glorious, and our praise all the more deserved!

## ACTIVITY

You will need 10 to 15 pieces of paper, big enough to write one word on; something to write with.

Explain that you are going to look together at why Jesus went to the cross, and what happened when Jesus rose again.

Together make a list of as many sins as you can think of (lying, hatred, bitterness, murder, etc.) by writing each one on a separate piece of paper. Assure people that by suggesting them, they're not owning up to anything!

Place them one by one in the middle of the room, forming a cross. As you lay each one down, say something to the effect of 'On the cross, Jesus took the punishment for . . .' and name the sin. Point out that this cross represents every sin that has ever been committed, including our own. Allow a moment for people to take that in.

Read out 2 Corinthians 5:21:

*God made him who had no sin to be sin for us, so that in him we might become the righteousness of God.*

Say: 'At that moment, Jesus became sin for us; even the Father could not look upon his beloved Son. At that moment, the price was paid.'

But it didn't end there. When God raised Jesus from the dead, the *power* of every sin was broken. (Begin tearing up each piece of paper, saying something like 'He broke the power of . . . in our lives'.)

Then begin to celebrate the victory of his resurrection with prayers and songs.

## KEY SCRIPTURES

John 11:25–26

*Jesus said to her, 'I am the resurrection and the life. He who believes in me will live, even though he dies; and whoever lives and believes in me will never die.'*

Jesus' resurrection means we will be with him for ever.

### 2 Timothy 1:10

*[God's grace] has now been revealed through the appearing of our Saviour, Christ Jesus, who has destroyed death and has brought life and immortality to light through the gospel.*

### 1 Corinthians 15:54–55

*Death has been swallowed up in victory. Where, O death, is your victory? Where, O death, is your sting?*

### Revelation 1:18

*I am the Living One; I was dead, and behold I am alive for ever and ever! And I hold the keys of death and Hades.*

Death has been defeated! Because Jesus was raised to life, death holds no fear for us, for it cannot separate us from him.

### Colossians 3:3

*For you died, and your life is now hidden with Christ in God.*

### Romans 8:11

*And if the Spirit of him who raised Jesus from the dead is living in you, he who raised Christ from the dead will also give life to your mortal bodies through his Spirit, who lives in you.*

When we become Christians, our old sinful nature dies, and we become new creations in Christ. And the same Spirit that raised Jesus from the dead is now active in us, giving us life and working to make us more like him.

## SONGS (Disc 7)

1. He has risen
2. Jesus we celebrate Your victory
3. Here is the risen Son
4. At Your feet we fall

## PRAYER

Lord, we are amazed and humbled that you should give up your life for us. But we are filled with joy that you rose again, defeating death, taking captivity captive, and that you now reign as King of kings and Lord of lords. Thank you that the power of sin is broken in our lives, and we are raised with you – and all because of your sacrifice. We worship you, the Name above all names. Amen.

## APPLICATION

If the power of sin has been broken in our lives, why do we still sin? The reasons for this might be many and varied, and the Bible doesn't teach that the power of the resurrection and new birth makes sin an impossibility.

But the big difference is, *now we have a choice*. Before we became Christians, we were slaves to sin. When we were saved, we died to sin, and received a new nature. Now we are slaves to righteousness (Romans 6:18). We have the power of God working in us, and God will give us the grace we need to live godly lives for him.

Ask God to help you live this week in the victory of his resurrection power.

# 32. The Return of Christ

## INTRODUCTION

As Christians, we are all aware that one day Jesus will return. However, if we're honest, we are often so preoccupied with our daily routine that we don't give it much thought. We certainly don't seem to have that sense of excitement that the apostle John attributes to the Spirit and the Bride at the close of Revelation: 'Amen. Come, Lord Jesus!'

And yet we are to live in the expectation that Jesus will come back soon. On several occasions in the gospels Jesus exhorts his disciples to be ready for his return.

## ACTIVITY

This activity is intended to help bring home to us the reality of Jesus' impending return. As you read the three passages, allow time for people to picture the scenes in detail, and to feel the emotion of each situation. You may even want to ask people to express their feelings and thoughts at the end of each passage.

Ask people to imagine the following three scriptures as scenes in a play. Encourage people to close their eyes if it helps them to visualize things better:

Scene 1 (John 14:3) – The disciples and Jesus are gathered in the upper room to celebrate the Passover. The meal is over, but Jesus is in serious, even sombre mood. He has washed their feet and told them that one of them will betray him, that Peter will deny him, and that he will shortly leave them. The disciples are shocked, puzzled, and anxious to know what all this means. Then Jesus says: 'And if I go and prepare a place for you, I will come back and take you to be with me that you also may be where I am.'

Scene 2 (Acts 1:9–11) – The last few days have been almost unbelievable. From the despair of Jesus' arrest, the shame of every single disciple deserting him, the horror of seeing the man who held all their hopes and beliefs brutally executed . . . to the shock and amazing joy of seeing him alive again – the same, but somehow different. And yet he's still talking about leaving. He takes them up to the Mount of Olives – a regular place for them to sit and talk – and then something remarkable happens:

*[Then] he was taken up before their very eyes, and a cloud hid him from their sight.*
 *They were looking intently up into the sky as he was going, when suddenly two men dressed in white stood beside them.*
 *'Men of Galilee,' they said, 'why do you stand here looking into the sky? This same Jesus, who has been taken from you into heaven, will come back in the same way you have seen him go into heaven.'*

Scene 3 (Revelation 1:7) – Just a normal day. You're at work, or at home, collecting the children, shopping, eating lunch. Suddenly you hear a loud, indescribable sound. There's a commotion outside as people are shouting to one another.

The daylight seems to be getting brighter and brighter. You run outside, and in the sky you see billowing clouds, and the light becomes so bright, you have to shield your eyes from the glare. And then you see, incredibly, in the middle of the clouds, the figure of a man . . .

*Look, he is coming with the clouds,*
  *and every eye will see him,*
*even those who pierced him;*
  *and all the peoples of the earth will mourn because of him.*

These are real scenes, in the real world. Two have already taken place, one is yet to happen. Although the prospect of the last scene may fill us with awe, it should not fill us with fear. It is the fulfilment of Jesus' promise to his followers, that he will return to take us home.

Let's praise the King of kings, who now sits at his Father's right hand, awaiting his call to come back for us.

## THANKSGIVING

- All your promises will be fulfilled, including your promise to return.
- You are coming back for your beloved Bride – that's us!
- Then we will see you face to face, and be with you for ever.
- In an instant you will bring to an end all the suffering and sin of this world.

## KEY SCRIPTURES

Matthew 24:36

*No-one knows about that day or hour, not even the angels in heaven, nor the Son, but only the Father.*

Lord, when you were on earth even you did not know the time of your return. Give us the ability to live each day with the faith and expectancy of your return.

Philippians 3:20–21

*But our citizenship is in heaven. And we eagerly await a Saviour from there, the Lord Jesus Christ, who, by the power that enables him to bring everything under his control, will transform our lowly bodies so that they will be like his glorious body.*

We do not belong to this world. One day we will be caught up with you, we will see you face to face, we will receive a new resurrection body – then we will have truly 'come home'.

Romans 8:22–23

*We know that the whole creation has been groaning as in the pains of childbirth right up to the present time. Not only so, but we ourselves, who have the firstfruits of the Spirit, groan inwardly as we wait eagerly for our adoption as sons, the redemption of our bodies.*

It's not just us; permeating the whole of nature is a sense of incompleteness, a longing for something more.

Revelation 22:17

*The Spirit and the bride say, 'Come!' And let him who hears say, 'Come!' Whoever is thirsty, let him come; and whoever wishes, let him take the free gift of the water of life.*

Lord, sometimes we lose our perspective, and live as if what happens here on earth is the only thing that matters. Put a hunger in our hearts for your return, and help us to discern what is of true importance in our daily lives.

SONGS (Disc 7)

5. Sound the trumpet
6. We have sung our songs (How long?)
7. Filled with compassion (For all the people who live on the earth)
8. O come, O come, Immanuel (*Instrumental*)

## PRAYER

Jesus, we are so glad that we know you, and that you have already revealed yourself to us as Saviour, King and Friend. We wait expectantly for the day when we will see you face to face, when the Bride and the Bridegroom will be united for ever.

We recognize that this isn't our home. May our words, our attitudes and our priorities reflect the fact that we are citizens of heaven. Amen.

## APPLICATION

If you knew Jesus was returning at this time tomorrow, how would you spend your last 24 hours on this earth? Given that no one knows the day or the hour – in other words, it could be tomorrow! – does this prompt you to rethink any of the priorities in your life?

*Part 3: The Holy Spirit and Our Life in God*

# 33. The Trinity

INTRODUCTION

The Trinity is central to our understanding of God. Although the Bible never uses the term as such, when all the strands of the Bible are brought together, it paints an irrefutable picture of one God, Father, Son and Holy Spirit – beautifully alluded to in the opening remarks of many of Paul's letters.

Some people struggle to understand the idea of the Trinity – that God could be three persons, yet one being. This activity may help to convey the way the three facets of the Trinity intertwine into one holy, loving God.

ACTIVITY

You will need some white card, some coloured pens and a few pencils. (An activity for groups that like making things!)

In advance, prepare some circles cut from the white card, about six inches in diameter. Divide each circle into three equal segments by drawing lines from the centre to the edge.

Divide people into groups of two or three, and give each group a circle, explaining that the three sections of the card represent the Father, Son and Holy Spirit. Each group writes names or characteristics of Father, Son and Holy Spirit in the appropriate part of the circle, *using a different colour for each section*. For example, in the Father section people might write: 'creator, provider, judge, omnipotent' in blue; and in the Holy Spirit section they might write: 'new wine, omnipresent, gentle, powerful', etc. in red.

After about ten minutes, each group tells the rest what they have written in the different sections. Then, give each group a pencil, which should be pushed through the centre of the card circle to form a sort of spinning top. Spin the tops and notice how the three colours blur together, representing the one God (Hear, O Israel, the Lord your God is one God) but three distinct persons.

## THANKSGIVING

- For the many facets of your character.
- For the love of the Father, the blood of the Son, and the indwelling of the Holy Spirit.
- That your Spirit is our guarantee of eternal salvation.

## KEY SCRIPTURES

Galatians 4:6

*Because you are sons, God sent the Spirit of his Son into our hearts, the Spirit who calls out, 'Abba, Father.'*

2 Corinthians 1:21–22

*Now it is God who makes both us and you stand firm in Christ. He anointed us, set his seal of ownership on us, and put his Spirit in our hearts as a deposit, guaranteeing what is to come.*

You reign in the heavens; yet you live in me. You are the righteous King of creation; yet by the Spirit I can call you 'Father'. You will one day judge the earth; yet your Spirit is my guarantee of eternal life.

1 Peter 1:2

*[To God's elect,] who have been chosen according to the fore-knowledge of God the Father, through the sanctifying work of the Spirit, for obedience to Jesus Christ and sprinkling by his blood.*

Thank you that every aspect of your character is at work in me – I'm chosen by the Father, justified through the Son, and I'm being sanctified by the Spirit.

John 14:26

*But the Counsellor, the Holy Spirit, whom the Father will send in my name, will teach you all things and will remind you of everything I have said to you.*

You didn't leave your disciples. You made a way to be with each one of us wherever we go!

John 3:34–35

*For the one whom God has sent speaks the words of God, for God gives the Spirit without limit. The Father loves the Son and has placed everything in his hands.*

When we worship, we participate in a loving, worshipping relationship between Father, Son and Holy Spirit. The Father loves the Son, who gives glory to the Father. The Spirit joins our spirit in worship to the Father and the Son. Loving worship permeates everything that God does!

## SONGS (Disc 7)

 9. Praise God from whom all blessings flow
10. I lift my hands (I will serve no foreign god)
11. Let Your living water flow
12. I give You all the honour (*Instrumental*)

## PRAYER

Thank you, Lord, for the richness of your character: Father, Saviour, Helper, Friend – so much more than we could ever dream of. Thank you that you reign in heaven, yet you live in us; you are the awesome God who lives in unapproachable light, yet you made yourself the scorn of men, the complete expression of your sacrificial love for us, so that we could live in you, and you could live in us. Teach us more of the vastness and wonder of the Trinity. Amen.

## APPLICATION

A rejection of the doctrine of the Trinity is probably the most common feature of Christian cults and heresies. Discuss for a few moments why it is so important to understand that Father, Son and Holy Spirit are all God.

Here are a few thoughts on the subject:

1   If Jesus were not God, we (along with others in the Bible) would be committing idolatry by worshipping him.
2   Only God could carry the burden of the sins of the whole world on himself, and only God could be trusted to deliver salvation. Therefore Jesus must be God.

3　The Bible clearly teaches that Jesus is God!

4　The Holy Spirit is omnipresent (Psalm 139:7–8).

5　He is omniscient (1 Corinthians 2:10–11).

6　He is a personal being: he is grieved, he comforts, he teaches and guides.

7　We baptize into his name, along with the Father and the Son.

# 34. The Names of God

NOTE: The following three chapters look at the names of God, the names of Jesus, and the names of the Holy Spirit. They can be used completely independently, as both the introduction (below) and application (no. 36) apply equally to all of them. However, you might want to use them across consecutive meetings as a kind of worship study. If covering these themes in this way, it might be helpful to use the same large sheet of paper for each activity, dividing it into three columns, so that the names of the Trinity are displayed side by side.

As you work through the names, encourage people to respond in praise and thanksgiving for what that name means to them. Allow time for the truths expressed in these names to take hold of people, as the effect can be life-changing.

These lists are by no means comprehensive. Feel free to add other names you know from the Bible, or to miss some out from the list here.

## INTRODUCTION

If you happen to have a book of people's names and their meanings, keep it handy.

Ask: 'Do you know what your name means?' (Look up the names of those who don't.) 'Do you know why you were

called by that name?' 'Did anyone have a (pleasant!) nick-
name when they were younger?' 'Does anyone (just for fun)
have an unusual middle name?'

The choosing of names seems to have had greater
significance in Bible times than now. A name might indicate
a person's destiny (Abraham = father of a multitude), or a
physical attribute (Esau = hairy), or even the state of a
nation (Ichabod = the glory has departed). So perhaps you
shouldn't be so upset about your middle name after all!

When it comes to God, names take on an even greater
significance. He has many names in the Bible, but they all
accurately express his nature and character. You can rely on
his names to be true. And more than that: they are powerful!
When we use his name in faith, we are acknowledging him
to be what his name means.

Let's come before him, speaking out the glorious names of
the Lord.


## ACTIVITY

You will need several small pieces of paper, a pen, and a large
sheet of paper (left-over wallpaper is ideal) attached to the
wall.

Write out some or all of the following names of God with
their references on separate pieces of paper, and hand them
out. Get each person in turn to read out the name, then look
up and read out the scripture. Write the name on the large
sheet of paper. Briefly discuss what the name tells us about
the character and work of God, and encourage someone to
respond with a short prayer of praise.

The names of God:

El-Roi – The God who sees me (Genesis 16:13)
El-Shaddai – Almighty God (Genesis 17:1–2)
Yahweh – I AM that I AM (Exodus 3:14)
Jehovah-Jireh – The Lord will provide (Genesis 22:14)
Jehovah-Shalom – The Lord is peace (Judges 6:24)
Jehovah-Tsidkenu – The Lord our righteousness (Jeremiah
    23:5–6; 33:16)
Ancient of Days (Daniel 7:9)
The Rock (Isaiah 26:4)
Fortress (Psalm 18:2)
Sun (Psalm 84:11)
Refiner (Malachi 3:3)
Shepherd (Psalm 23:1)
Our Father (Matthew 6:9)
Father of compassion (2 Corinthians 1:3)
Father of glory (Ephesians 1:17)
Abba Father (Romans 8:15)

## THANKSGIVING

- You are all-seeing, all-powerful, all-conquering, and yet
  you are our Father.
- Every name you have is a promise we can depend on.
- You never change: what was true for your people down
  through history is true for us now.

## SONGS (Disc 7)

13. Among the gods
14. Salvation belongs to our God
15. God of glory
16. I worship You, Almighty God

## PRAYER

Father, thank you for your wonderful names, which remind us of your protection, your provision, and the fullness of your salvation. Above all, we are so glad to be able to call you Father, and to know we are accepted into your family for ever. Amen.

# 35. The Names of Jesus

ACTIVITY

You will need several small pieces of paper, a pen, and a large sheet of paper (left-over wallpaper is ideal) attached to the wall.

Write out some or all of the following names of Jesus with their references on separate pieces of paper, and hand them out. Get each person in turn to read out the name, then look up and read out the scripture. Write the name on the large sheet of paper. Briefly discuss what the name tells us about the character and work of Jesus, and encourage someone to respond with a short prayer of praise.

The names of Jesus:

Alpha and Omega (Revelation 1:8; 22:13)
Bread of life (John 6:35, 48)
Good Shepherd (John 10:14)
Lamb of God (John 1:29, 36)
Light of the world (John 8:12)
Prince of peace (Isaiah 9:6)
Word (John 1:1; 5:7)
Resurrection and the life (John 11:25)

King of kings (1 Timothy 6:15; Revelation 17:14)
I AM (Exodus 3:14; John 8:58)

## THANKSGIVING

- These are more than titles: each one is a promise of life to us.
- Your names have power, because of the authority given to you by the Father.
- You are the name above all names.

## SONGS (Disc 7)

17. There is a voice (Jesus, Friend of sinners)
18. All my days (Beautiful Saviour)
19. Friend of sinners
20. There is a Redeemer

## PRAYER

Jesus, we are excited and awed by the greatness of your names. Thank you that each one means life, strength and eternal security to us. We praise you, the King of kings, who became the suffering servant for our salvation. Amen.

# 36. The Names of the Holy Spirit

You will need several small pieces of paper, a pen, and a large
sheet of paper (left-over wallpaper is ideal) attached to the
wall.

Write out the following names of the Holy Spirit with
their references on separate pieces of paper, and hand
them out. Get each person in turn to read out the name,
then look up and read out the scripture. Write the name
on the large sheet of paper. Briefly discuss what the
name tells us about the character and work of the Holy
Spirit, and encourage someone to respond with a short
prayer of praise.

The names of the Holy Spirit:

Breath of the Almighty (Job 33:4)
Comforter/Counsellor (John 14:16, 26; 15:26)
Spirit of Christ (Romans 8:9; 1 Peter 1:11)
Spirit of the Father (Matthew 10:20)
Spirit of grace (Zechariah 12:10; Hebrews 10:29)
Spirit of prophecy (Revelation 19:10)
Spirit of adoption (Romans 8:15)
Spirit of wisdom (Isaiah 11:2; Ephesians 1:17)

Spirit of holiness (Romans 1:4)
Spirit of understanding (Isaiah 11:2)

## THANKSGIVING

* You dwell with us, guiding, comforting and empowering us.
* You are our 'deposit', our guarantee of what God has promised.
* You produce fruit in our lives, making us more like Jesus.

## SONGS (Disc 8)

1. Peace like a river
2. Breathe on me, breath of God
3. O God of burning cleansing flame (Send the fire)
4. Spirit of the living God (*Instrumental*)

## PRAYER

Holy Spirit, we thank you for your wonderful work in us, bringing a greater understanding and experience of salvation with each day. Thank you that you comfort, strengthen and guide us every step of our lives. Teach us to hear your promptings better, and rely on your power to live lives of righteousness, peace and joy. Amen.

## APPLICATION

Names were sometimes added to or changed in keeping with a new phase or role in life: Abram to Abraham, Jacob to Israel, Simon to Peter. The name was to express something of the nature or role of the person who owned it.

Isaiah 43:1 says: 'Fear not, for I have redeemed you; I have summoned you *by name*; you are mine' (emphasis added). God knows each one of us completely. And not only that, he knows what we have the potential to become, and what we will become.

In the light of this, putting to one side for a moment your earthly name, what name do you think he might use for you? By what name would you like to be called? Pray together that you might receive his grace to fulfil all that he wants you to be.

# 37. Chosen by God

## INTRODUCTION

Many Christians are under the mistaken impression that we are Christians simply because we chose to be. 'Deciding to follow Jesus', or 'making a decision for Christ' are commonly used phrases; but although they may be true in terms of our response to him, they are only that – a response to his original call. The Bible is clear: we didn't choose him – he chose us!

What an amazing thought: that the Creator of the universe should handpick us before we were even born, to belong to him for ever! Let's rejoice in the security of knowing we are his children.

## ACTIVITY

Use the Ephesians 1 passage below as a basis for thanksgiving. Read each section out separately, encouraging individuals to share any thoughts they have on it, and to pray a short prayer of thanks.

Ephesians 1:3–6

*Praise be to the God and Father of our Lord Jesus Christ, who has blessed us in the heavenly realms with every spiritual blessing in Christ.*

In blessing us, God held nothing back; every spiritual blessing you can think of – love, joy, acceptance, security, power, peace, righteousness – is ours in Christ!

*For he chose us in him before the creation of the world to be holy and blameless in his sight.*

God's choosing of us is not based on anything we've done, because we were chosen even before the world was made. And we were chosen not just to be saved, but to be completely clean before him, because of the blood of Jesus. This is not a vain hope or a lofty ideal; this is God's plan for each one of us, accomplished by the same power that raised Jesus from the dead.

*In love he predestined us to be adopted as his sons through Jesus Christ, in accordance with his pleasure and will.*

Not only chosen, but brought into God's own family, with all the love, security and inheritance that comes from being a child of God. And God didn't do it reluctantly or out of duty – he did it for his own pleasure.

*. . . to the praise of his glorious grace, which he has freely given us in the One he loves.*

All the goodness of God has been given to us freely and without measure. Can we even begin to appreciate how much he loves us?

## THANKSGIVING

- Considering the selfishness and arrogance of human beings, it's amazing that you should even consider saving anyone.
- Our salvation depends on you, not us.
- Your choosing of us does not depend on who we are, or what we have done – you loved us before we were even born.
- Not only are we chosen, but we are adopted into your family – beloved sons and daughters of God.

## KEY SCRIPTURES

### John 6:44

*No-one can come to me unless the Father who sent me draws him, and I will raise him up at the last day.*

We have been drawn by the Father. When we begin to realize that salvation is God's idea, it takes away the fear of not being good enough to attain it or keep it.

### John 15:16

*You did not choose me, but I chose you and appointed you to go and bear fruit – fruit that will last. Then the Father will give you whatever you ask in my name.*

We are called not just to receive salvation, but to bear fruit, to become more like Christ. And to do it, God promises all the resources we need to be good 'fruit-bearers', if only we will ask.

Ephesians 2:10

*For we are God's workmanship, created in Christ Jesus to do good works, which God prepared in advance for us to do.*

God's workmanship: he is fashioning us, shaping us, tenderly and patiently carving out the image of Jesus in our lives, that we might be a testimony of God's love and faithfulness to those around us.

**See also**

1 Peter 1:2 – the whole of the Trinity is involved in our salvation.

Romans 9:14–18 – God's choosing of us is sovereign, not dependent on any effort or desire on our part.

1 Corinthians 1:27–29 – in case we think we're anything special.

SONGS (Disc 8)

5. Be free in the love of God
6. I am a new creation
7. You did not wait for me (I'm forever grateful)
8. I will sing of the Lamb

PRAYER

Lord, we can't begin to understand why you should choose us, but we are so grateful that you did. Thank you for the security of knowing we are yours, the delight of knowing we are blameless in your sight, and the power at work in us to make us more like Jesus. Amen.

## APPLICATION

Read out (if you haven't already) Ephesians 2:10 above. We are created to do good works. It's what we're called to do; we have all the resources of God to do it; and God's committed to the task. Ask: 'What good works has God lined up for each one of us this week? How will we recognize them when they come along?'

Pray with one another to hear God's voice this week, and to recognize those opportunities for good works.

# 38. Fruit of the Spirit

## INTRODUCTION

Read out Galatians 5:22–23

*But the fruit of the Spirit is love, joy, peace, patience, kindness, goodness, faithfulness, gentleness and self-control. Against such things there is no law.*

When we think of the fruit of the Spirit, we tend to run through this list from Galatians with a tinge of guilt and sense of failure. We might feel that occasionally we exhibit one or two of these characteristics, but it quickly passes! Generally we fall well short of what is required.

But if we think like this, we've missed the point. Paul is not presenting us with rules; as he says, there's no law that can make this fruit grow. No; he's encouraging us to 'walk in the Spirit' (v. 25), and fruit will grow as a natural consequence.

Where do you think this list comes from? It's a description of God, of course! He has all these characteristics – and more – in abundance. He has given us his Spirit not to live up to a checklist, but to make us more and more like him. So the fruit of the Holy Spirit is simply becoming more like Jesus.

Let's celebrate the God who overflows with wonderful qualities, and gives us the grace and the power to be like him.

## ACTIVITY

You will need:

1  a 'tree', i.e. a branch of some kind, with plenty of twigs on it to hang things from, planted in a plant-pot;
2  pieces of paper cut out in the shape of leaves or fruit, enough for one per person (or perhaps two if your group is quite small), with some way of hanging them from the twigs (a hole punched in the corner, a loop of string attached, etc.);
3  something to write with.

Hand out the pieces of paper, and ask people to write down one aspect of the character of God they really appreciate (love, gentleness, mercy, etc.). Encourage them to think of an incident or time in their lives when this aspect of God's nature was very evident to them.

Go round the room, asking each one to share what they've written, and the incident they've remembered; and as they share, get them to hang the 'fruit' from the tree.

After everyone has finished, begin to worship God with prayers, songs and readings, focusing on the wonderful attributes that are displayed on the tree.

## THANKSGIVING

We thank you, Lord, for:

• your love
• your faithfulness
• your holiness
• your compassion
• your grace

- your mercy
- your forgiveness
- your fatherhood
- your gentleness
- your power
- your creativity

## KEY SCRIPTURES

### Romans 5:8

*But God demonstrates his own love for us in this: While we were still sinners, Christ died for us.*

Love without conditions. No guarantee of love returned. Just selfless, risky love that cost everything.

### 1 John 1:9

*If we confess our sins, he is faithful and just and will forgive us our sins and purify us from all unrighteousness.*

Your forgiveness requires no penance, no punishment on our part. The price has been paid, and all we have to do is to be humble enough to receive it.

### John 1:14

*The Word became flesh and made his dwelling among us. We have seen his glory, the glory of the One and Only, who came from the Father, full of grace and truth.*

Jesus, you showed us what grace and truth look like in a human being. You were guided, comforted and strengthened by the same Spirit that lives in us.

## SONGS (Disc 8)

9. Let there be joy
10. Rejoice!
11. I want to be a tree that's bearing fruit
12. May my delight (Psalm 1)

## PRAYER

Lord, you are greater than our wildest imaginings – more loving, more forgiving, more gracious, more merciful than we could ever know. Thank you that your wonderful qualities were demonstrated in Jesus, in whom the fullness of the Godhead dwelt. There was no better way to show us what you are like, or what we mean to you.

We want the fruit of your character to be evident in our lives. Keep us from striving, but teach us to draw on your resources continually and to abide in you by the power of the Holy Spirit within us. Amen.

## APPLICATION

God wants us to be like him. Just as the tree represents God's various qualities, so we are to be like a fruitful tree. Ask people to consider the tree before them once again, encouraging them to choose one 'fruit', one aspect of God's character where they feel they are weak, and pray for God to grow that particular fruit in their lives.

Encourage people to expect God to change them in the coming days and weeks in the area they have identified.

## 39. The Promises of God 1

NOTE: This idea is in two parts, and will work best if spread across two consecutive weeks. The first part explores why we can trust God's promises. The second part looks at some of the promises themselves.

### INTRODUCTION

So often we are guilty of using words cheaply: 'I'll phone you . . . we'll have you round for dinner sometime . . .' They so easily trip off the tongue, yet too often our promises don't materialize.

God is completely different. There are no idle words that come from his mouth. Every statement he utters, every promise he makes, is utterly dependable. We can trust completely in everything he has said.

### ACTIVITY/KEY SCRIPTURES

How good are *we* at keeping promises? Ask people to think of (and share, if they can!) the last time they broke a promise.

Let's think of reasons why we fail to live up to our promises:

- We forget.
- Circumstances change.
- We promise something we could never deliver anyway.

The good news is that God always keeps his promises! He never forgets, or makes a rash promise, or is thwarted by circumstances. We can rely on his promises. Why?

## They are fulfilled in Christ

2 Corinthians 1:20

*For no matter how many promises God has made, they are 'Yes' in Christ. And so through him the 'Amen' is spoken by us to the glory of God.*

Jesus is the fulfilment of every promise made by God: indeed, he is the very Word of God. He fulfilled the Old Testament prophecies about the Messiah; he was living proof of God's character in his life; and by his death and resurrection, he accomplished God's promise of salvation – fully, finally and completely.

## He knows the beginning from the end

Psalm 33:13–15

*From heaven the Lord looks down*
  *and sees all mankind;*
*from his dwelling place he watches*
  *all who live on earth –*
*he who forms the hearts of all,*
  *who considers everything they do.*

God knows everything about us – our past, present and future – because he formed us in the first place! We can be assured that he will fulfil his promises, because he can never be caught off balance or taken aback by circumstances.

**His words have creative power**

Hebrews 1:3

*The Son is the radiance of God's glory and the exact represen-*
*tation of his being, sustaining all things by his powerful word.*

Jesus' powerful word sustains the very universe we live in; we
can surely trust the words of his promises.

**God is sovereign and eternal**

Mark 13:31

*Heaven and earth will pass away, but my words will never pass*
*away.*

The words of Jesus are eternal. They are more enduring and
dependable than the earth itself. Let's give thanks to the One
who is committed to fulfilling his promises to us.

THANKSGIVING

- You are trustworthy in every word you have said.
- Your desire as a Father is to give us every good thing.
- Your very words have power in our lives.

SONGS (Disc 8)

13.  I'm gonna trust in God
14.  I walk by faith
15.  I cry out (Good to me)
16.  Our confidence is in the Lord

## PRAYER

Thank you, Lord, for your complete dependability. Your words are power and life to us, and we put our trust in every word you have spoken. Amen.

## APPLICATION

Read out James 3:1–12 together. It is a sobering reminder of the power of the tongue, and the potential damage it can cause.

How careful are we in what we say to others? Does our speech usually build up or tear down? Are we quick to compliment and slow to criticize, or the other way round?

Take a moment to consider how we might use our tongues righteously this week.

# 40. The Promises of God 2

## INTRODUCTION

We know that we can trust in God's promises. His words are true and dependable, for they rely on both his awesome power and his passionate love towards us. And, if that wasn't enough, they are reinforced – made 'yes and amen' – in the death and resurrection of Jesus.

## ACTIVITY

You will need several pieces of paper, each with a scripture promise written out (you can choose from those below, or find your own). The more you can do, the more impact it will have when the papers are laid out together.

Hand out the pieces of paper. Ask each person to read theirs out, and to share (if they can) what that promise means to them. Encourage them to be specific about how the promise impacts feelings or circumstances in their lives (perhaps by asking questions).

After everyone has finished, get them to lay out all the pieces of paper on the floor or on a table in the middle of the room, and begin to thank God together for his wonderful promises to us. Encourage individuals to speak out their thanks to God for a specific promise.

## Scripture promises

2 Corinthians 6:18

*I will be a Father to you,*
*    and you will be my sons and daughters,*
*says the Lord Almighty.*

John 11:25–26

*Jesus said to her, 'I am the resurrection and the life. He who believes in me will live, even though he dies; and whoever lives and believes in me will never die.'*

John 3:16

*For God so loved the world that he gave his one and only Son, that whoever believes in him shall not perish but have eternal life.*

John 4:13–14

*Jesus answered, 'Everyone who drinks this water will be thirsty again, but whoever drinks the water I give him will never thirst. Indeed, the water I give him will become in him a spring of water welling up to eternal life.'*

John 6:35

*Then Jesus declared, 'I am the bread of life. He who comes to me will never go hungry, and he who believes in me will never be thirsty.'*

John 6:47

*I tell you the truth, he who believes [in me] has everlasting life.*

John 8:31–32

*To the Jews who had believed him, Jesus said, 'If you hold to my teaching, you are really my disciples. Then you will know the truth, and the truth will set you free.'*

John 15:7

*If you remain in me and my words remain in you, ask whatever you wish, and it will be given you.*

Matthew 7:7–8

*Ask and it will be given to you; seek and you will find; knock and the door will be opened to you. For everyone who asks receives; he who seeks finds; and to him who knocks, the door will be opened.*

Hebrews 13:5

*Keep your lives free from the love of money and be content with what you have, because God has said, 'Never will I leave you; never will I forsake you.'*

SONGS (Disc 8)

17. In every circumstance
18. We're looking to Your promise of old (Send revival, start with me)
19. I know not why God's wondrous grace
20. Just like You promised (*Instrumental*)

PRAYER

Lord, thank you for the many promises you make. Thank you that they are more than comforting words; they are truths upon which we can build our lives. Teach us to live by your promises, not by our feelings or expectations. Amen.

## APPLICATION

Consider 2 Corinthians 7:1:

*Since we have these promises, dear friends, let us purify ourselves from everything that contaminates body and spirit, perfecting holiness out of reverence for God.*

What do we have to do (or not do) this week to help us come into the fullness of God's promises for us?

# 41. Grace

## INTRODUCTION

Grace is the fundamental activity of the Bible: it is God's love in action. People have attempted to define it in various ways, two of the most memorable being 'God's unmerited favour', and 'G-R-A-C-E – God's Riches At Christ's Expense'.

Whatever definition you prefer, at the heart of grace is (1) our inability to earn God's favour, and (2) God's free gift of salvation, which does not depend on anything we have done, but on Christ alone.

The more we think about this, the more amazing it becomes. We could never earn God's salvation, no matter how devout or pious we are. But we don't need to! It has been won for us, and now it has been given to us, freely and lavishly. And the result is that we want to serve him with all that we have, and worship him wholeheartedly.

## ACTIVITY

You will need a piece of paper, and something to write with.

Have different people read out some of the scriptures below, and after each one, as a group pick out the words that describe us without God's grace, and those that describe what we are and have with grace. Write them out in two columns. So for example, your list may look like this:

**Without grace**
- Sinners
- Fall short
- Powerless
- Ungodly

**With grace**
- Righteousness
- Redemption
- Loved
- Adopted as sons
- Forgiveness
- Riches of God's grace

Take a few moments to discuss together what each of these words means. Make it as practical and specific as possible. Then, one after another, begin to thank God for the amazing change his grace has made in our lives, and praise him for the gift of his Son by which grace was made possible.

## THANKSGIVING

- Your grace is ours because of the victory of Christ.
- Our righteousness has nothing to do with it.
- Grace is a gift – a gift can't be earned!
- You continue to pour out grace on our lives day after day.

## KEY SCRIPTURES

Romans 3:23–24

*All have sinned and fall short of the glory of God, and are justified freely by his grace through the redemption that came by Christ Jesus.*

Rich and poor, head of state and vagrant, convict and judge – we all have one thing in common: every one of us needs the grace of God in our lives.

Romans 5:6–8

*You see, at just the right time, when we were still powerless, Christ died for the ungodly. Very rarely will anyone die for a righteous man, though for a good man someone might possibly dare to die. But God demonstrates his own love for us in this: While we were still sinners, Christ died for us.*

God didn't wait for a spark of righteousness, a sign perhaps that we were marginally better than other people. In fact, we didn't even have the power to receive it! His grace is a complete, unselfish, unmerited act of love.

John 1:16–17 (NASB)

*For of His fulness we have all received, and grace upon grace. For the Law was given through Moses; grace and truth were realized through Jesus Christ.*

Grace upon grace – it's a never-ending flow of grace, of one blessing after another, from the immeasurable fullness of Christ himself.

**See also**

Proverbs 3:34 – God looks for humility.

Ephesians 1:5–8 – his grace for us is just right for each one of us, because it comes with wisdom and understanding.

Ephesians 2:8–9 – we don't need to earn it; we just need to believe it.

## SONGS (Disc 9)

1. Just as I am
2. Amazing grace
3. Wonderful grace
4. God of grace

## QUOTES

Heaven goes by favour. If it went by merit, you would stay out, and your dog would go in.

Mark Twain

Grace isn't cheap – just paid for. The only thing it costs us is admitting we're completely broke. And for some, that's too big a price to pay.

Stuart Townend

## PRAYER

Lord, we are amazed by your grace: the King of kings, who willingly endured what we deserve in order that we might receive what you deserve – and all for the joy set before you, the joy of bringing us into your glorious kingdom! No wonder you are given the name that is above every other name! Amen!

## APPLICATION

As we have seen, grace doesn't stop at salvation. It is the ongoing blessing of God in our lives for every situation, all our hopes and disappointments, every success and failure. In fact, God tells the apostle Paul, 'My grace is sufficient for you, for my power is made perfect in weakness' (2 Corinthians 12:9).

It's not our areas of strength that exhibit the power of God, but our areas of weakness. Where do you need more of the grace of God in your life right now? Pray together in twos for specific breakthroughs of God's power in our weakness.

# 42. Heaven

## INTRODUCTION

Pastors and worship leaders have been known to end worship times with 'Well, at least in heaven we won't have to stop.' However, for many of us, nothing could be more terrifying than the thought that heaven will be an eternal church service!

The Bible doesn't give a lot of detail about what heaven will be like – in fact, Jesus talks more about hell than he does heaven. However, what is clear is that it is a place of great light and beauty, of glory, peace, wholeness and, above all, the place where God dwells with his people.

Perhaps the best way to think of it is, it's better than the best place you could possibly imagine.

## ACTIVITY

Read John 14:2 below. Ask everyone to describe their 'dream house'. Allow people to indulge themselves as they describe all the luxuries and extravagances they would like to have. We can safely presume that the place Jesus is preparing for us is at least as good as our dream house – so we may have to do without our dream house until we get the ultimate one.

## THANKSGIVING

- We will be face to face with you, Lord.
- There will be no more pain, injustice or sorrow.
- We will be free from all sin.
- We will join with Christians from every age and every land.
- It will be a place of peace, joy and complete fulfilment.

## KEY SCRIPTURES

### John 14:2

*In my Father's house are many rooms; if it were not so, I would have told you. I am going there to prepare a place for you.*

Jesus knows everything about us. He became a man, and experienced every aspect of our humanity for himself. Now he's gone to prepare the place for us himself. So there's no doubt that it will be perfect.

### 1 Corinthians 13:12

*Now we see but a poor reflection as in a mirror; then we shall see face to face. Now I know in part; then I shall know fully, even as I am fully known.*

Face to face with you – nothing secret, no more confusion or doubt. Lord, we have tasted enough to be sure that knowing you fully will be complete satisfaction and joy.

### Revelation 7:9

*After this I looked and there before me was a great multitude that no one could count, from every nation, tribe, people and language, standing before the throne and in front of the Lamb. They were wearing white robes and were holding palm branches in their hands.*

God has no favourite countries or races – his plan of salvation has not skipped a single tribe or people group. One day we will worship shoulder to shoulder with brothers and sisters from every strand of humanity.

Revelation 7:16–17

*Never again will they hunger,*
  *never again will they thirst.*
*The sun will not beat upon them,*
  *nor any scorching heat.*
*For the Lamb at the centre of the throne will be their shepherd;*
  *he will lead them to springs of living water.*
*And God will wipe away every tear from their eyes.*

It's hard to imagine an existence without any of the pain or suffering that seems so much part of ordinary life. And yet one day God's comfort of us, his people, will be complete, and suffering and sin will be a thing of the past.

**See also**

Revelation 22:1–5 – a place of living water, fruitfulness and light.

Isaiah 11:6 – there is complete security and safety.

2 Timothy 4:8 – there's a crown of righteousness awaiting all those who are eagerly expecting the Lord's return.

SONGS (Disc 9)

5. There's a place (Because of You)
6. O my soul arise
7. Sing a song of celebration (We shall dance)
8. O the valleys shall ring (*Instrumental*)

QUOTE

> We're not just human beings having a temporary spiritual experience. But we're spiritual beings having a temporary human experience.
>
> Teilhard de Chardin, French priest

APPLICATION

There's a line in the carol 'Once in royal David's city' which describes the heavenly picture of Jesus on the throne: 'When like stars His children crowned, / All in white shall *wait around*'. It's a rather unfortunate expression now, as it implies that the saints are a little bored, waiting for something to happen. One thing is sure: heaven will not be boring! We'll be serving Jesus, loving him, and reigning with him for ever.

The early church seemed very conscious of their eternal destiny, so much so that they were ready to suffer and even give up their lives for the gospel (see Acts 5:33, 40–42; 7:54–60). Paul himself was torn between staying on earth and going to be with the Lord (Philippians 1:21–24).

Do we hold our time on earth that lightly? How should a proper view of heaven affect the way we live on earth? How should we reorder the priorities of our lives?

## 43. Hope

### INTRODUCTION

The gospel is full of hope – Jesus is described in the Scriptures as our hope (1 Timothy 1:1), and we are to '*overflow* with hope by the power of the Holy Spirit' (Romans 15:13).

But our hope is not just blind optimism, and it's not a particular personality trait. It is rooted in the character of God – his goodness, faithfulness and unfailing love – in all his promises and in his salvation provided for us through his Son Jesus. We have both eternal hope, and hope in the everyday situation, as in the hymn 'Great is thy faithfulness': 'strength for today, and bright hope for tomorrow'.

### ACTIVITY

Sometimes we think that as Christians nothing will ever go wrong for us, and we are surprised when we face hardship. Recount the following story to the group and discuss:

Many of us know the hymn 'It is well with my soul', but we may not know the story behind it. In 1874 a French steamer *Ville de Havre* was returning from America to France. On board was a Mrs Spafford, the wife of a Chicago lawyer, and her four children. In the middle of the Atlantic the steamer collided with a sailing vessel and began to sink.

Mrs Spafford hurried her children on deck and prayed with them that God would either save them, or make them ready to die. The steamer sank within half an hour, and nearly all on board were lost, the children among them. Mrs Spafford was rescued and brought to Cardiff where she cabled her husband, Horatio, with the message 'Saved alone.' He came immediately to bring his wife home to Chicago, and wrote the hymn out of his experience:

> When peace like a river attendeth my way
> When sorrows like sea-billows roll
> Whatever my lot, Thou hast taught me to know
> It is well, it is well with my soul.
>
> Horatio G. Spafford (1828–88)

What does this story teach us about hope?

Begin to worship the sovereign Lord, the One on whom our hope depends.

## THANKSGIVING

- Our hope is not in vain; we have a faithful God, a risen Saviour, and an indwelling Counsellor who are our guarantee of what has been promised.
- Circumstances and feeling do not change our hope, for it is based on what we know.
- Our hope is Jesus, and all he has promised. He has defeated death; so whom shall we fear?

## KEY SCRIPTURES

### 1 Peter 1:3

*Praise be to the God and Father of our Lord Jesus Christ! In his great mercy he has given us new birth into a living hope through the resurrection of Jesus Christ from the dead.*

Our hope is not an idea: it's a person. The fact that Jesus did not stay dead, but was raised to life, defeating death, means that we can be certain of our hope of eternal life.

### Colossians 1:27

*To them God has chosen to make known among the Gentiles the glorious riches of this mystery, which is Christ in you, the hope of glory.*

Our hope springs from our union with Christ.

### Romans 15:13

*May the God of hope fill you with all joy and peace as you trust in him, so that you may overflow with hope by the power of the Holy Spirit.*

Hope is not just something we do; it is fuelled by the power of the Holy Spirit.

### Psalm 43:5

*Why are you downcast, O my soul?*
  *Why so disturbed within me?*
*Put your hope in God,*
  *for I will yet praise him,*
  *my Saviour and my God.*

Our hope is not dependent on our circumstances or our feelings. Hope comes through what we know. So we can still rejoice in our hope, even when we are downcast and troubled.

**See also**

Hebrews 10:19–25 – our hope is based on the faithfulness of God.

SONGS (Disc 9)

9. It's rising up
10. Before the throne of God above
11. What a friend I've found (Jesus, Friend for ever)
12. I will sing the wondrous story (*Instrumental*)

PRAYER

Lord, sometimes it seems as if we live in such a hopeless world, full of people without hope. But you have changed everything for us. Whatever our situation, we know that your promises are true, and that you are faithful.

We do not look to our circumstances, to warm feelings, or to material things for our hope, but to the foundation of our hope, Jesus himself. Because he lives, our hope is steadfast and certain. Amen.

APPLICATION

Pray with anyone who feels they are in a seemingly hopeless situation – long-term illness, for example. Pray for renewed faith and peace in God, and pray according to the way you feel God leading, and the faith he is giving you. If there is insufficient time, you could arrange to pray on another occasion, if appropriate with church leaders, who can anoint the sick person with oil.

Also, if appropriate, offer to pray, either now, or later in private, with anyone who does not feel they have 'a certain hope' about their salvation.

In both instances, be sure to follow up these situations.

# 44. Mercy

## INTRODUCTION

Mercy is a common theme of both the Old and New Testaments. But do we really understand what mercy is?

As Dr Martyn Lloyd-Jones points out, mercy is not just pity to those in need; it is pity plus action. The Good Samaritan didn't just feel compassion, as others might have done at seeing an injured man lying in the road. He showed mercy, by dressing his wounds, and taking care of him.

When the Bible says God is merciful, it doesn't just mean he feels for us. He has already done something to redeem our situation. And mercy is not at odds with justice. His mercy didn't involve 'letting us off the hook'; it involved putting the full punishment for our sin on Jesus. Mercy has triumphed over judgement (James 2:13), not by excusing our sin, but by fulfilling the requirements of justice – with mercy to spare.

Let's worship the One whose compassion led him to perform the greatest act of sacrifice in history.

## ACTIVITY

Consider together the impact of God's mercy on your life:

* What kind of state were you in before he saved you?
* What first caused you to respond to the gospel?

- How and when did you actually become a Christian?
- What was the reaction of those around you (family, friends)?
- Where do you think you might have ended up without Christ?
- What single thing are you most grateful to God for?

The answers to some of these questions might be more dramatic for some than for others. Point out that it's not the drama of the conversion, but the richness of your life in Christ now that matters.

## THANKSGIVING

- Your mercy caused you to act, sending Jesus as a ransom for our sin and rebellion.
- You acted in mercy before we were even prepared to admit our need of it.
- Your mercy still flows towards us, bringing forgiveness for sin, strength for weakness, and restoration for guilt.

## KEY SCRIPTURES

Psalm 116:1

*I love the Lord, for he heard my voice;*
  *he heard my cry for mercy.*

God hears our cry, and responds with mercy.

Psalm 51:1

*For the director of music. A psalm of David. When the prophet Nathan came to him after David had committed adultery with Bathsheba.*

*Have mercy on me, O God,*
  *according to your unfailing love;*
*according to your great compassion*
  *blot out my transgressions.*

Even when our sin is grave, your response to repentance is mercy and restoration.

Matthew 5:7

*Blessed are the merciful,*
  *for they will be shown mercy.*

God wants us to respond to his acts of mercy towards us by showing mercy to others. It's not that God's mercy is conditional on us being merciful: the only condition of receiving God's mercy is repentance. But a failure to show mercy to others indicates a hardness of heart, and a lack of real repentance. The heart that cannot show mercy, has not learnt to receive it.

Romans 12:1

*Therefore, I urge you, brothers, in view of God's mercy, to offer your bodies as living sacrifices, holy and pleasing to God – this is your spiritual act of worship.*

The proper response to God's mercy is devotion.

SONGS (Disc 9)

13.  Oh the mercy of God
14.  Overwhelmed by love
15.  You are merciful to me
16.  I don't know why (All I know)

## PRAYER

Lord, we were far off, but you brought us near. We were in darkness, but you shone your light into our hearts. We were in rebellion against you, but you brought conviction and repentance. Why did you do it? Because you are merciful. And you continue to shower us with mercy by your acts of kindness and love to us. Goodness and mercy really are following us all the days of our lives! Amen.

## APPLICATION

God has shown great mercy towards us. How good are we at showing mercy to others?

Are we quick to forgive those who hurt us?

Do we harbour resentment when others seem to be favoured over us?

Do we give time and financial resources to those around us who are in need?

Take a moment to pray together, asking God to reveal the full extent of his mercy towards us, that we might show greater mercy to others.

# 45. Forgiveness

## INTRODUCTION

Forgiveness is central to the gospel. Because of our sin, we deserve to spend eternity separated from God. But because of God's great love, he has made a way, through the sacrifice of Jesus, for us to be forgiven. Let's praise him for the life-changing power of forgiveness, which is freely given to us, but cost him everything.

## TESTIMONY

Chris Carrier of Florida was abducted when he was ten years old, burned with cigarettes, stabbed with an ice pick, shot in the head, and left to die. Remarkably, he survived, though he lost the sight in one eye. No one was ever arrested.

Recently, a man confessed to the crime, and Carrier, now a youth minister, went to see him. He found a 77-year-old ex-convict, David McAllister, frail and blind in a nursing home. Carrier began to visit him regularly, reading the Bible and praying with him, paving the way for McAllister to make a profession of faith.

Carrier says:

> While many people can't understand how I could forgive David McAllister, from my point of view I couldn't *not* forgive him. If

218

I'd chosen to hate him all these years, or spent my life looking for revenge, then I wouldn't be the man I am today, the man my wife and children love, the man God has helped me to be.

'Christian Reader' in *Leadership*, January/February 1998

## ACTIVITY

You will need two pieces of cloth or string, and two volunteers.

Ask someone to read out the following verses:

### Matthew 6:14–15

*For if you forgive men when they sin against you, your heavenly Father will also forgive you. But if you do not forgive men their sins, your Father will not forgive your sins.*

### Mark 11:25

*And when you stand praying, if you hold anything against anyone, forgive him, so that your Father in heaven may forgive you your sins.*

Ask one volunteer to play the role of someone who needs the forgiveness of another person. Gently bind this person's wrists together with the string or cloth. They then simply ask the other volunteer: 'Please forgive me,' offering their bound wrists to be untied. The other person says every time: 'No, I won't.' Each time the person refuses to forgive, wrap the other string or cloth around *their* wrists until they too are (not too tightly!) bound.

Ask: 'What does this show us about refusing to forgive?'
Now read and consider Luke 23:33–34:

*When they came to the place called the Skull, there they crucified him, along with the criminals – one on his right, the other on his left. Jesus said, 'Father, forgive them, for they do not know what they are doing.'*

It is ironic to note that while the person who refused to forgive has hands bound together, the One forgiving the most hideous crime in world history willingly had his hands nailed apart.

## THANKSGIVING

- You endured the greatest humiliation, rejection and suffering that humanity could throw at you, and yet you forgave.
- Your forgiveness is complete, final and continuous for the repentant sinner.
- Your example sets us free to be able to forgive others.

## KEY SCRIPTURES

Hebrews 8:12

*For I will forgive their wickedness
    and will remember their sins no more.*

God forgives *and* forgets!

Psalm 103:12 (NASB)

*As far as the east is from the west,
    So far has He removed our transgressions from us.*

Once God has forgiven us, guilt over past sin need never come back to haunt us.

## 1 John 1:9 (NASB)

*If we confess our sins, He is faithful and righteous to forgive us our sins and to cleanse us from all unrighteousness.*

As we allow him, through confession and repentance, God will not only forgive, but cleanse us from those attitudes and past hurts that cause us to stumble, so that we can live lives of freedom and righteousness.

## SONGS (Disc 9)

17. Lift Him up
18. O Lord, Your tenderness
19. You rescued me
20. I know a place (At the cross)

## QUOTE

Forgiveness is the perfume that the trampled flower casts upon the heel that crushed it.

From *14,000 Quips and Quotes* by E. C. McKenzie (Baker, 1980)

## PRAYER

Father, thank you for the power of forgiveness. Thank you that it has transformed us from guilty, blind slaves to sin, to forgiven, free, beloved children of God. Let the full power of your forgiveness continue to lead us to fullness of life in Christ. Amen.

## APPLICATION

Forgiveness is freely given to us. But it requires us to have the same attitude to others that God has to us.

Are there people we need to forgive in order to come into the good of God's forgiveness for us? If so, consider once again what you have been forgiven, and the attitude of forgiveness that Jesus showed to his persecutors, and then speak forgiveness to those who have sinned against you. (It may be appropriate for this to be done later in private with a trusted friend or counsellor.)

# 46. I Believe

## INTRODUCTION

The creeds are the distilled statements of belief upon which our faith is based. Although many churches do not regularly recite a creed together in a service, the statements of, say, the Nicene or Apostles' Creed would readily be embraced by the whole of orthodox Christianity. They are the fundamentals of our faith.

## ACTIVITY

For those who regularly use creeds in their services, this is an opportunity to pause and reflect on the wonderful truths that are often quickly rattled through on the way to the sermon or the Communion. For those who don't, it's a rare opportunity to express the basics of our faith together. For a few, it will be a rare opportunity to learn them.

If you have time, it would be helpful to write out the creed on a sheet of paper beforehand, so it can be read together. Otherwise, each line could be read out by one person, then repeated by the others.

First, try reading out together the whole creed without the comments below. Then read out one line at a time. After each line, read out (or adapt) the thoughts below, or simply leave a moment of silence. Perhaps one person could lead in a prayer of thanks after each line.

### I believe in God the Father

God *and* Father; the voice of One who to this day calls stars into being, tenderly calls me 'son'.

### Maker of heaven and earth

All I can see, hear, touch, smell, is his idea. Vastness and detail, physical and emotional, all began in his mind. And the Maker of me – with all my faults, gifts, failings – still looks and says it's 'very good'.

### And in Jesus Christ his only Son our Lord

No other plan, no other Son in case it all went horribly wrong. When God dreamed up the plan of salvation, he put everything he had into it. For a brief time heaven was bereft of its full glory, as the beloved Son gave up everything to become the champion of sinners.

### Who was conceived by the Holy Spirit

Miraculous . . . almost unbelievable – God becomes a seed, a fertilized egg in the womb of a teenage girl. Immanuel – God with us, one of us.

### Born of the virgin Mary

Surely God should come with a blinding light, a blast of trumpets? Instead, a couple of private angelic visitations, a dream or two, a solitary star ignored by almost everybody. The veil momentarily lifted for a handful of shepherds. And somewhere, in the backwater town of a backwater country, a baby's cry from an animal shelter, signalling the safe arrival of the Saviour of the world.

*Suffered under Pontius Pilate*
No safe, comfortable birth. Now a shockingly slow, agonizing road to death. A self-important official, deciding just another man's fate. Shall I, or shan't I? Sensing something not right, but opting out when the pressure was on. Have him beaten, have him disposed of. Yet this decision was destined from the moment the earth was made, prophesied in detail hundreds of years before. By those wounds I am healed.

*Was crucified, died and was buried*
No reprieve, no heavenly intervention. Only a dark sky. His life ebbed away, and his followers, his friends, his mother, were left with a corpse. Day turned to night, and nothing had changed. It really was all over – finished.

*The third day he rose again from the dead*
Sorrow turns to incredulity, then to joy, then to awe. This man, the one we ate with, walked with, talked with, lived with – he really is the glorious Son of the living God! Powerful, glorious, wonderful – even the final enemy, death itself, could not keep him from us!

*He ascended into heaven, and sitteth at the right hand of God the Father Almighty*
Totally victorious! Heaven is even more glorious than before, now it has a Man who has won through, dealt with the sin that kept us lost, separated and cold towards God, and opens the way for me to be restored to him.

*From thence he shall come to judge the quick and the dead*
For God to offer himself up in this way, the stakes must be high. Pilate's choice is echoed in the heart of every person

who has ever lived. Shall I, or shan't I? Salvation or judgement? And because I acknowledge that my righteousness is as filthy rags before the Righteous One, I choose his righteousness as my own.

### I believe in the Holy Spirit

I'm not left alone. I have the Spirit of Jesus, the mind of Christ, the Counsellor – he's all I need for holy living, and he's the down payment on what's to come. Can't wait!

### The holy catholic [universal] church

Many churches, one body. Many leaders, one Shepherd. Many nations, races, languages, dialects – all united, equal and holy in him.

### The communion of saints

The most difficult, dull, stupid Christian I can think of is my brother or sister. How dare I reject what God has accepted! How dare I judge what God has embraced! We're not joined by church affiliation, affection, similar interests, or need – we're joined by Christ.

### The forgiveness of sins

The worst thing I've ever done – the nasty comment, the violence, the murderous thought – I repent of, and it's forgiven *and* forgotten. Yes, really! If I sin today, he has a right to be surprised; as far as he's concerned, it's the first one I've ever committed.

### The resurrection of the body, and the life everlasting

I quite like this body, but it lets me down. Not just weak knees and toothache, but, like an inquisitive bloodhound, it pulls me into blind alleys and tricky terrain if I don't pull on the lead and show it who's boss. But one day, I'll have a body that will match my spirit, and that will be total freedom. And I'll have it for ever.

## SONGS (Disc 10)

1. I believe in God the Father
2. There is power in the name of Jesus
3. I believe there is a God in heaven
4. To God be the glory (*Instrumental*)

## PRAYER

Thank you, Lord, that these things are totally, reliably true. Thank you that we have a solid foundation for our lives, and a reason for the hope we have. Help us to keep building our lives on the truth of who you are. Amen.

## APPLICATION

Many today would say that the only important thing about belief is that you believe it. Why is objective truth important? How can truth help us in our daily lives?

# 47. Thankfulness

## INTRODUCTION

We are probably all aware that we need to be thankful. Some of us do it grudgingly (remember as a child being forced to say a 'thank-you' after each meal?); some of us do it habitually ('Praise the Lord!' or 'Thank you, Lord' seems to trip off some people's tongues without them even thinking about it).

But we need to remember that thanksgiving is more than a phrase. It's an attitude. In being thankful to God, we are recognizing our total dependence on him – he puts breath in our lungs and food on our table, gives salvation for our souls, brings comfort, hope and strength.

As we regularly take time to consider what God is like, what he does, and what he is able to do, we find we begin to nurture a response of thankfulness. It's not an attitude of 'always looking on the bright side', or denying the reality of a difficult situation. But it's a response that recognizes God's continual goodness to us, whatever the circumstances.

## ACTIVITY

You will need a pack of thank-you notelets – you can either buy them, or make your own.

Before you begin to pray or sing your thanksgiving, try the following.

Many of us will have written thank-you notes to relatives after Christmas and birthdays (often reluctantly, out of laziness!). Explain that we are going to write a thank-you note to God.

Distribute a notelet to each person, and give them about five minutes to write down in the form of a short letter ('Dear God . . .') something they are thankful for today, whether small or large. Writing silently for five minutes often focuses our minds much more than talking or listening to others.

Ask if anyone feels able to share what they have written (don't pressure people into this). Then use what is shared as a basis for the group to give thanks to God.

## THANKSGIVING

- For his faithfulness and provision every day of our lives.
- For the indescribable gift of Jesus.
- For his sovereignty over every situation we face.
- For his overwhelming love.
- For the gift of the Holy Spirit, who lives in us.

## KEY SCRIPTURES

Psalm 105:1

*Give thanks to the Lord, call on his name;*
  *make known among the nations what he has done.*

Part of thankfulness is declaring how good he is to those who don't know him.

2 Corinthians 9:15

*Thanks be to God for his indescribable gift!*

The greatest cause of thanksgiving for us is Jesus himself.

Colossians 3:17

*And whatever you do, whether in word or deed, do it all in the name of the Lord Jesus, giving thanks to God the Father through him.*

Lord, let every conversation, every comment, every action somehow reflect your grace and mercy towards us. Let it not be self-seeking, attempting to justify ourselves, or insensitive to others.

Philippians 4:6

*Do not be anxious about anything, but in everything, by prayer and petition, with thanksgiving, present your requests to God.*

Teach us to ask, instead of worry. And let our prayers always reflect what you have given, as well as what we need.

Colossians 2:6–7

*So then, just as you received Christ Jesus as Lord, continue to live in him, rooted and built up in him, strengthened in the faith as you were taught, and overflowing with thankfulness.*

Lord, teach me to overflow!

## SONGS (Disc 10)

5. Give thanks
6. Here I am (I will always love Your name)
7. Thank You for the cross
8. In the Lord

## QUOTE

Many people quench the Spirit by being down in the mouth rather than rejoicing, by planning rather than praying, by murmuring rather than giving thanks, and by worrying instead of trusting in him who is faithful.

Cameron Townsend
quoted in *The Speaker's Sourcebook* (Zondervan, 1975)

## PRAYER

Lord, so often we take for granted your great goodness to us. We are quick to complain, and slow to be grateful. And yet, when we consider your great grace and mercy towards us, all we can do is thank you.

We are for ever in your debt, but you count no debt against us. We were far away from you, but you brought us near. We were not fit to be in your presence, but you made us clean. We were dead in our sins, but you made us alive in Christ. In response to your overwhelming goodness towards us, teach us to develop an attitude of thankfulness that pervades our words and actions. Amen.

## APPLICATION

Colossians tells us to do everything in the name of Jesus with thankfulness. Ask people to pick two daily activities they enjoy, and two they dislike. How can an attitude of thank-fulness come into those activities? How does a thankful atti-tude affect the way we do those things?

## 48. The Body of Christ

### INTRODUCTION

We are the body of Christ. It sounds an astonishing, even slightly blasphemous, idea, yet it's thoroughly biblical. When someone becomes a Christian, they enter a huge family of believers in which God resides, and through which he accomplishes his purposes.

Whether we like it or not, we are all related. And God is building us together for a greater plan – that his glory might be seen on the earth. His body, the church, is the instrument through which people from every tongue, tribe and nation will be gathered, and added to his body. We are all part of a living, growing spiritual dwelling place for God.

### ACTIVITY

You will need a piece of paper, or preferably a picture from a magazine, cut or torn into random shapes. You will need the same number of pieces as people in the group. (If you have fewer than ten people, give everyone two pieces each.)

Give each person a piece of the picture, and explain that you want to put the original back together again. Someone will offer to put a piece on the table or floor first and then carry on until the paper has been recreated.

233

Then read 1 Corinthians 12:12–30 (or parts of the passage). Reflect together on how the activity with the pieces of paper demonstrates the body of Christ – perhaps ask these questions:

- Are the shapes all the same?
- What happens if I take one piece away?
- Do the shapes fit perfectly? (Yes and no – you can see the joins but they are still in the right place and represent the original.)
- What would happen if everybody wanted to place their piece of paper on the table first instead of working together?

Spend some time thanking God that he has placed different-shaped people like you in just the right way to be Christ's body on earth.

## THANKSGIVING

- For the Holy Spirit shared in our hearts
- For God's purpose to use us together in his plans
- For one another's friendship, gifts and love
- For the importance of every part of the body
- For our need of one another

## KEY SCRIPTURES

1 Corinthians 3:16

*Don't you know that you yourselves are God's temple and that God's Spirit lives in you?*

There are no longer any holy places or holy things – only holy people. Jesus now dwells in us, his body, by the Holy Spirit.

Ephesians 2:21

*In [Jesus] the whole building is joined [KJV: fitly framed] together and rises to become a holy temple in the Lord.*

Fitly framed together. Jesus moulds each one of us to be just the right shape, so we can be joined together as a holy temple. I am the shape I am because you are the shape you are – the fit might not be perfect yet, but he's working on it!

Ephesians 4:2–6

*Be completely humble and gentle; be patient, bearing with one another in love. Make every effort to keep the unity of the Spirit through the bond of peace. There is one body and one Spirit – just as you were called to one hope when you were called – one Lord, one faith, one baptism; one God and Father of all, who is over all and through all and in all.*

We need to bear with one another, because God is still shaping each one of us. And we are learning to be joined together. If there is no unity, there is no body.

**See also**

1 Peter 2:5 – we are living stones, being built into a spiritual house.

SONGS (Disc 10)

9. An army of ordinary people
10. Jesus loves the church (Can you hear Him singing?)
11. Lord we come (Join our hearts)
12. Christ is made the sure foundation (*Instrumental*)

## PRAYER

Thank you for the value you place on us, causing each one to be an active part of your body here on earth. Thank you that you are our head, directing us, and building us together through the bond of the Spirit. Teach us more of what it means to be a body of believers, supporting, honouring and loving one another as you love us. Amen.

## APPLICATION

Groucho Marx's old adage 'I would never want to join a club that would have me as a member' could easily be applied to the church. There's no such thing as a perfect church, so long as people are involved in it. Often we become exasperated with others, and think how much better our church would be without them. But although it may appear to us that some people are oddly shaped living stones, we're probably only irritated because God's using them to knock *us* into shape!

Who is God using right now to shape you more into the image of Jesus? Pray for a soft heart to allow the grace of God to change you.

# 49. The Lord's Prayer

## INTRODUCTION

The Lord's Prayer is probably the best-known prayer in the world. However, it's not actually *the Lord's* prayer as such; it's more accurately the Lord's instructions on *how to pray*. The primary intention is not really for us just to recite the words; it's a guideline given by Jesus for us to understand how to approach God in praise and prayer. Let's use it as a basis for our worship together now.

## ACTIVITY

Begin by reciting the Lord's Prayer together (you may need to decide first whether you're going to use the 'modern' or 'traditional' version). If you think that some people may not know it, you may want to write it out on a large sheet beforehand. Alternatively, you could all read from the same version of the Bible (Matthew 6:9–13).

Then read it out together again, a line at a time. Leave space after each line for quiet reflection, or share the thoughts below. Encourage people to speak out their worship and prayers at each point.

*Our Father, who art in heaven*
You are not a distant sovereign, but a Father – ruling and reigning from a throne, but dispensing love and mercy to all who turn to you.

*Hallowed be your name*
May your name, all you represent, be held in honour and awe, as you deserve. May everything I am and do speak of your glory.

*Your kingdom come*
May all your kingdom values – love for one another, caring for the poor, righteous living, healing and deliverance – invade my society, my town, my street.

*Your will be done on earth as it is in heaven*
In heaven, your perfection, your faithfulness, your total care, your *best* find full and free expression. On earth, these things are resisted by fallen men and women, and they are blind and lost as a result. Soften hard hearts, and use me to be an instrument of righteous decisions.

*Give us this day our daily bread*
You hear what we desire, but you know what we need. Peace of mind doesn't come from having tomorrow's bread today; it comes from trusting you for new mercies every morning.

*And forgive us our trespasses*
I have sinned. Yet you promise the repentant sinner forgiveness – full, complete, free. What's past is past; it has no hold on me.

*As we forgive those who trespass against us*
Forgiveness is tough to do, but the alternative binds my transgressor and cripples me. I may feel justified in refusing to forgive; but if I in my sinfulness insist on justifying myself, how can I be justified by you, the sinless One? Where the heart is concerned, forgiveness can never be a one-way street.

*And lead us not into temptation*
You know my limits, and my weaknesses. When I begin to wander down that familiar path towards sin – whether through habit, weakness, or sheer wilfulness – speak to my heart, that core which hungers for righteousness and intimacy with you.

*But deliver us from evil*
I know I'm probably not my own worst enemy. So when the fiery darts come, and the lion prowls, give me faith to trust in the certain promise of your protection.

*For yours is the kingdom, the power, and the glory, for ever and ever. Amen.*

SONGS (Disc 10)

13. Our Father who art in heaven (Millennium prayer)
14. We will give ourselves no rest (Knocking on the door of heaven)
15. Can a nation be changed?
16. To Him who loves us

## PRAYER

Thank you for these wonderful words. May they be to us more than a familiar quotation, but a description of our lives as we dedicate ourselves to follow you. Amen.

## QUOTES

Many writers seem to have something clever to say about temptation. Here are a few quotes from *The Speaker's Sourcebook* that may be of value:

Some people feel that the only way to handle temptation successfully is to yield to it.

Anon.

Temptation is the tempter looking through the keyhole into the room where you are living; sin is drawing back the bolt and making it possible for him to enter.

J. Wilbur Chapman

Some temptations come to the industrious, but all temptations attack the idle.

C.H. Spurgeon

No one can honestly or hopefully be delivered from temptation unless he has himself honestly and firmly determined to do the best he can to keep out of it.

J. Ruskin

## APPLICATION

'Lead us not into temptation.' How well do we know ourselves? Are we aware of our weaknesses, and the circumstances that make us vulnerable to temptation? Ask people privately to identify an area of their lives where they often fall. What practical things could we do to make ourselves less vulnerable?

# 50. The Lord's My Shepherd

## INTRODUCTION

God as a shepherd is a picture used in both the Old and New Testaments. The analogy is in danger of passing us by in modern Western society, where the job of shepherd is rare to behold. Suffice to say, to be a shepherd in the dry land of Palestine was an exhausting job. Shepherds constantly had to watch over their flocks, regularly taking them to sources of fresh water, finding and returning strays, fighting off wild animals that threatened the flock, counting the sheep or goats in at the end of the day, and watching over them at night. God's care for us is that complete, every day of our lives.

## ACTIVITY

Read out this meditation on Psalm 23. Ensure people are comfortable and not distracted. They might find it helpful to close their eyes. You also may find unobtrusive instrumental background music helps. Leave time between each line for people to meditate on what's been said.

Psalm 23:1–6

*The Lord is my shepherd* – the shepherd is totally responsible for his sheep. He knows them by name, he feeds them, guides them, and defends them with his life. Lord, your commitment to me is complete – the Shepherd has already laid down his life for me.

*I shall not be in want* – you have given me everything I need. All the strength, all the patience, all the wisdom, all the passion, all the love that Jesus exhibited in his life is there for me, too.

*He makes me lie down in green pastures, he leads me beside quiet waters* – in this busyness and pressure, you promise rest. Filling every day with relentless work, shouting at the children, worrying about the bills, might be my way of dealing with things, but it's not yours. I want the peace of your presence to be part of my life.

*He restores my soul* – feeling weary, dry, beaten up by the pressures, is part of life. It's even part of the Christian's life. That's why I need to be restored regularly in my inner being.

*He guides me in paths of righteousness for his name's sake* – Lord, thank you that I'm going somewhere. I'm not just stuck in the sheep-pen waiting for the rapture. And thank you that for every situation I can think of, no matter how hopeless it appears, there's always a right way to walk, a right path to take.

*Even though I walk through the valley of the shadow of death, I will fear no evil, for you are with me; your rod and your staff, they comfort me* – God, I confess that sometimes I've thought you got it wrong, and told you so. There I am in the dark valley, waiting patiently for the cavalry to appear on the horizon, for the sound of the helicopter that's going to airlift me out of here. And all you say is, 'Keep walking.' A gentle rod in the back is not necessarily my ideal picture of comfort, but it tells me you're with me in this, and it's all I need to know.

The valley of the shadow of death – it's the one path we know we're all going to walk one day. Thank you that it's only a shadow; and the light beyond it is indescribably beautiful.

*You prepare a table before me in the presence of my enemies –* you know I'd prefer a quiet table in the corner for dinner. But enjoying the delights of God in full view of a world that hates you, at least it shows them what they're missing, and the feast becomes an invitation. Extolling the virtues of the local restaurant is one thing; the outdoor smell of a barbecue is quite another.

*You anoint my head with oil; my cup overflows* – drenched inside and out! Your blessing on my work for you, and your refreshing for my inner being.

*Surely goodness and love will follow me all the days of my life, and I will dwell in the house of the Lord for ever* – I couldn't ask for two better bodyguards. Even when the path isn't clear, or I've deliberately chosen to explore a hazardous cliff edge, goodness and love are close behind. And I can still hear your voice. It thrills me now, and it's a sound I'm going to hear and delight in for ever.

**See also**

Psalm 28:9 – you carry us on your shoulders.

John 10:11 – you give your life for us.

Matthew 18:12–14 – you care for each one of us.

John 10:14 – we can hear your voice.

## SONGS (Disc 10)

17. The Lord's my Shepherd
18. God of heaven
19. Father I come to You (Unending love)
20. The King of love my Shepherd is (*Instrumental*)

## PRAYER

Father, thank you for the completeness of your care for me. Thank you that you supply me with everything I need, you come even closer when I stray from the path, and you bless me with every spiritual blessing – not because I've earned it, but because it's Jesus' reward, given to me. I know I am safe in your hands, for ever. Amen.

## APPLICATION

We all find ourselves walking through dark valleys from time to time – they may be valleys of pressure, depression, illness, loss, fear – all things that can make us feel that the Shepherd is far away from us.

What is our response to these situations? Do we turn away from God, or turn towards him? Consider how we might train ourselves to stay close to him when things are difficult. This may include developing the habit of time alone with God, strengthening our relationships with others, learning to trust him in the bad times as well as the good.

# Index of Themes

*Locators refer to theme numbers, not page numbers*

# Index of Bible References

*Locators refer to theme numbers, not page numbers*

# Songs of Fellowship
## for Small Groups . . .

### . . . the complete resource for small group worship

*Kingsway are delighted to announce a major new initiative to help resource small groups everywhere to worship together:*

Songs of Fellowship for Small Groups –
## THE SONGSHEET

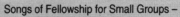

200 songs and hymns, carefully selected for their suitability in small group worship, set out in an easy-to-read A4 format. It's the perfect companion to *50 Worship Ideas for Small Groups* as all the songs suggested in the book are included in this songsheet!

Songs of Fellowship for Small Groups –
## THE CDS

You've got the words, now get the music! Many small groups lack competent musicians who can lead the worship with instruments, and increasingly groups are turning to pre-recorded music that can be listened to and sung along with.

This collection of 10 CDs features all 200 songs included in the songsheet and book. Each track is especially suitable for use in the small group. Most have a clear lead vocal and simple accompaniment for your group to sing to. But we've also included some beautiful instrumental tracks, ideal for reflective listening and meditation.

## AND THE BEST NEWS OF ALL . . .

All these elements are included in a single pack! Everything you need for small group worship in one place:

- The *50 Worship Ideas for Small Groups* book

- 10 songsheets (more available separately in packs of 10)

- The first 5 CDs in the series, contained in a sleek plastic ring-bound folder (the other 5 available separately by ordering direct)

- Everything contained in a specially designed, clear plastic carry-case, for easy transport and storage

For more details on this exciting new resource, contact your local Christian Bookshop, or contact us at Kingsway (Lottbridge Drove, Eastbourne, East Sussex BN23 6NT; tel: 01323 437700; email music@kingsway.co.uk).